Cram101 Textbook Outlines to accompany:

Human Motivation

Franken, 5th Edition

An Academic Internet Publishers (AIPI) publication (c) 2007.

Cram101 and Cram101.com are AIPI publications and services. All notes, highlights, reviews, and practice tests are prepared by AIPI for use in AIPI publications, all rights reserved.

You have a discounted membership at www.Cram101.com with this book.

Get all of the practice tests for the chapters of this textbook, and access in-depth reference material for writing essays and papers. Here is an example from a Cram101 Biology text:

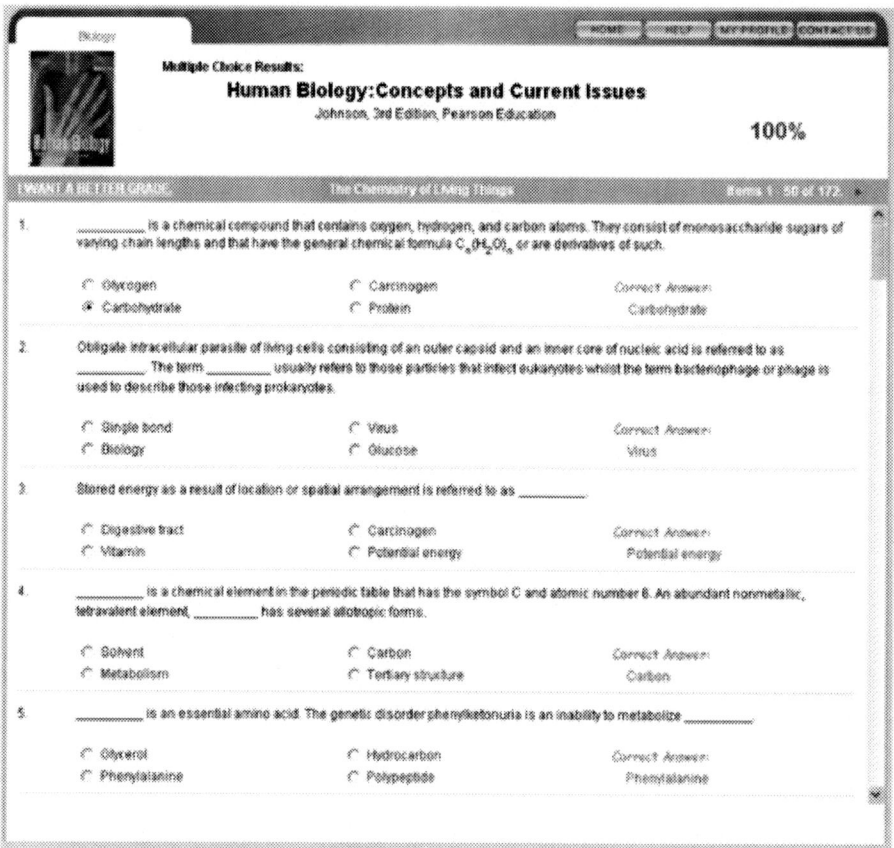

When you need problem solving help with math, stats, and other disciplines, www.Cram101.com will walk through the formulas and solutions step by step.

With Cram101.com online, you also have access to extensive reference material.

You will nail those essays and papers. Here is an example from a Cram101 Biology text:

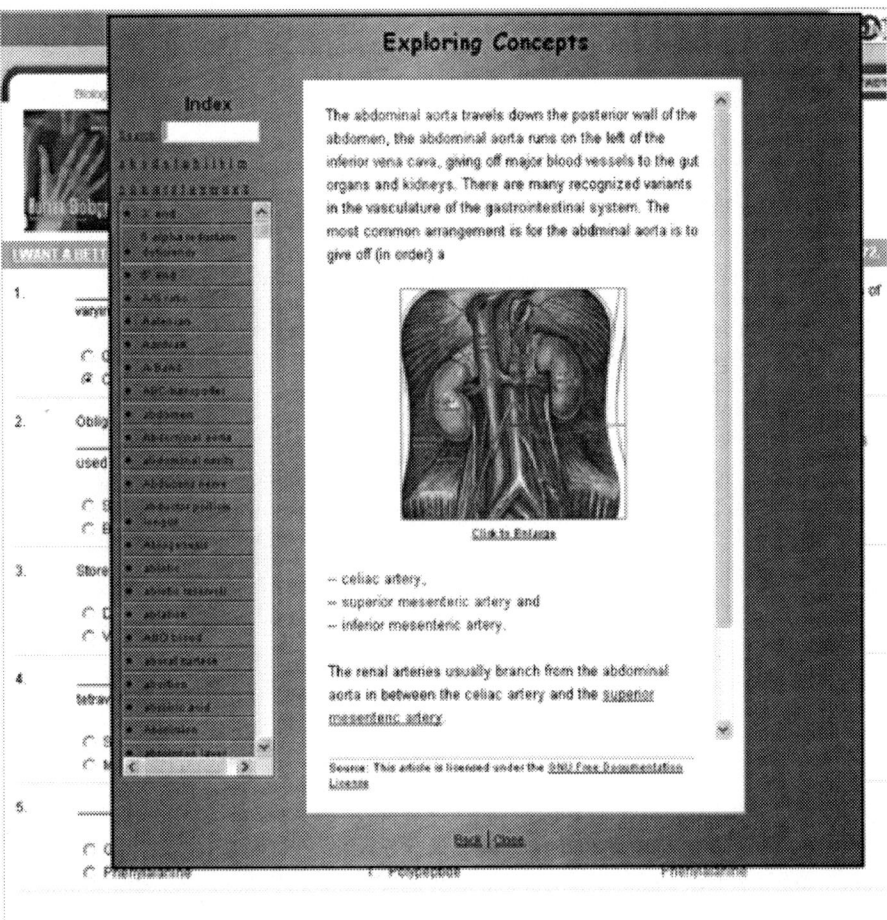

Visit **www.Cram101.com**, click Sign Up at the top of the screen, and enter DK73DW in the promo code box on the registration screen. Access to www.Cram101.com is normally $9.95, but because you have purchased this book, your access fee is only $4.95. Sign up and stop highlighting textbooks forever.

Learning System

Cram101 Textbook Outlines is a learning system. The notes in this book are the highlights of your textbook, you will never have to highlight a book again.

How to use this book. Take this book to class, it is your notebook for the lecture. The notes and highlights on the left hand side of the pages follow the outline and order of the textbook. All you have to do is follow along while your intructor presents the lecture. Circle the items emphasized in class and add other important information on the right side. With Cram101 Textbook Outlines you'll spend less time writing and more time listening. Learning becomes more efficient.

Cram101.com Online

Increase your studying efficiency by using Cram101.com's practice tests and online reference material. It is the perfect complement to Cram101 Textbook Outlines. Use self-teaching matching tests or simulate in-class testing with comprehensive multiple choice tests, or simply use Cram's true and false tests for quick review. Cram101.com even allows you to enter your in-class notes for an integrated studying format combining the textbook notes with your class notes.

Visit **www.Cram101.com**, click Sign Up at the top of the screen, and enter **DK73DW164** in the promo code box on the registration screen. Access to www.Cram101.com is normally $9.95, but because you have purchased this book, your access fee is only $4.95. Sign up and stop highlighting textbooks forever.

Copyright © 2007 by Academic Internet Publishers, Inc. All rights reserved. "Cram101"® and "Never Highlight a Book Again!"® are registered trademarks of Academic Internet Publishers, Inc. The Cram101 Textbook Outline series is printed in the United States. ISBN: 1-4288-0107-3

Human Motivation
Franken, 5th

CONTENTS

1. Themes in the Study of Motivation 2
2. Components of Motivation 14
3. Hunger and Eating 30
4. Passion, Love, and Sexual Behavior 38
5. Arousal, Attention, and Peak Performance 54
6. Wakefulness, Alertness, Sleep, and Dreams 68
7. Drug Use and Drug Addiction 84
8. Aggression, Coercive Action, and Anger 100
9. Emotions, Stress, and Health 114
10. Goal-Incongruent [Negative] Emotions 128
11. Goal-Congruent [Positive] Emotions 144
12. From Curiosity to Creativity 156
13. Need for Control, Mastery, and Self-Esteem 166
14. Self-Regulation of Motivation 174

Chapter 1. Themes in the Study of Motivation

Adolescence	The period of life bounded by puberty and the assumption of adult responsibilities is adolescence.
Personality	Personality refers to the pattern of enduring characteristics that differentiates a person, the patterns of behaviors that make each individual unique.
Attention	Attention is the cognitive process of selectively concentrating on one thing while ignoring other things. Psychologists have labeled three types of attention: sustained attention, selective attention, and divided attention.
Enzyme	An enzyme is a protein that catalyzes, or speeds up, a chemical reaction. Enzymes are essential to sustain life because most chemical reactions in biological cells would occur too slowly, or would lead to different products, without enzymes.
Learning	Learning is a relatively permanent change in behavior that results from experience. Thus, to attribute a behavioral change to learning, the change must be relatively permanent and must result from experience.
Prototype	A concept of a category of objects or events that serves as a good example of the category is called a prototype.
Survey	A method of scientific investigation in which a large sample of people answer questions about their attitudes or behavior is referred to as a survey.
Theories	Theories are logically self-consistent models or frameworks describing the behavior of a certain natural or social phenomenon. They are broad explanations and predictions concerning phenomena of interest.
Motivation	In psychology, motivation is the driving force (desire) behind all actions of an organism.
Cognition	The intellectual processes through which information is obtained, transformed, stored, retrieved, and otherwise used is cognition.
Anxiety	Anxiety is a complex combination of the feeling of fear, apprehension and worry often accompanied by physical sensations such as palpitations, chest pain and/or shortness of breath.
Sensation	Sensation is the first stage in the chain of biochemical and neurologic events that begins with the impinging of a stimulus upon the receptor cells of a sensory organ, which then leads to perception, the mental state that is reflected in statements like "I see a uniformly blue wall."
Evolutionary perspective	A perspective that focuses on how humans have evolved and adapted behaviors required for survival against various environmental pressures over the long course is called the evolutionary perspective.
Brain	The brain controls and coordinates most movement, behavior and homeostatic body functions such as heartbeat, blood pressure, fluid balance and body temperature. Functions of the brain are responsible for cognition, emotion, memory, motor learning and other sorts of learning. The brain is primarily made up of two types of cells: glia and neurons.
Nervous system	The body's electrochemical communication circuitry, made up of billions of neurons is a nervous system.
Feedback	Feedback refers to information returned to a person about the effects a response has had.
Goal-directed behavior	Goal-directed behavior is means-end problem solving behavior. In the infant, such behavior is first observed in the latter part of the first year.
Habit	A habit is a response that has become completely separated from its eliciting stimulus. Early learning theorists used the term to describe S-R associations, however not all S-R associations become a habit, rather many are extinguished after reinforcement is withdrawn.
Positive reinforcement	In positive reinforcement, a stimulus is added and the rate of responding increases.
Reinforcement	In operant conditioning, reinforcement is any change in an environment that (a) occurs after the

Chapter 1. Themes in the Study of Motivation

	behavior, (b) seems to make that behavior re-occur more often in the future and (c) that reoccurence of behavior must be the result of the change.
Negative reinforcement	During negative reinforcement, a stimulus is removed and the frequency of the behavior or response increases.
Extinction	In operant extinction, if no reinforcement is delivered after the response, gradually the behavior will no longer occur in the presence of the stimulus. The process is more rapid following continuous reinforcement rather than after partial reinforcement. In Classical Conditioning, repeated presentations of the CS without being followed by the US results in the extinction of the CS.
Intrinsic motivation	Intrinsic motivation causes people to engage in an activity for its own sake. They are subjective factors and include self-determination, curiosity, challenge, effort, and others.
Affect	A subjective feeling or emotional tone often accompanied by bodily expressions noticeable to others is called affect.
Gene	A gene is an ultramicroscopic area of the chromosome. It is the smallest physical unit of the DNA molecule that carries a piece of hereditary information.
Gender difference	A gender difference is a disparity between genders involving quality or quantity. Though some gender differences are controversial, they are not to be confused with sexist stereotypes.
Individual differences	Individual differences psychology studies the ways in which individual people differ in their behavior. This is distinguished from other aspects of psychology in that although psychology is ostensibly a study of individuals, modern psychologists invariably study groups.
Clinical psychologist	A psychologist, usually with a Ph.D, whose training is in the diagnosis, treatment, or research of psychological and behavioral disorders is a clinical psychologist.
Construct	A generalized concept, such as anxiety or gravity, is a construct.
Instinct	Instinct is the word used to describe inherent dispositions towards particular actions. They are generally an inherited pattern of responses or reactions to certain kinds of situations.
Humanistic theories	Humanistic theories focus attention on the whole, unique person, especially on the person's conscious understanding of his or her self and the world.
Humanistic	Humanistic refers to any system of thought focused on subjective experience and human problems and potentials.
Species	Species refers to a reproductively isolated breeding population.
Pineal gland	The pineal gland is a small endocrine gland. It is located near the center of the brain, between the two hemispheres and near the central switching point of the thalamic bodies. It is responsible for the production of melatonin, which has a role in regulating circadian rhythms.
Gland	A gland is an organ in an animal's body that synthesizes a substance for release such as hormones, often into the bloodstream or into cavities inside the body or its outer surface.
Insanity	A legal status indicating that a person cannot be held responsible for his or her actions because of mental illness is called insanity.
Tumor	A tumor is an abnormal growth that when located in the brain can either be malignant and directly destroy brain tissue, or be benign and disrupt functioning by increasing intracranial pressure.
Natural selection	Natural selection is a process by which biological populations are altered over time, as a result of the propagation of heritable traits that affect the capacity of individual organisms to survive and reproduce.
Genetics	Genetics is the science of genes, heredity, and the variation of organisms.
Mutation	Mutation is a permanent, sometimes transmissible (if the change is to a germ cell) change to the

Chapter 1. Themes in the Study of Motivation

Chapter 1. Themes in the Study of Motivation

	genetic material (usually DNA or RNA) of a cell. They can be caused by copying errors in the genetic material during cell division and by exposure to radiation, chemicals, or viruses, or can occur deliberately under cellular control during the processes such as meiosis or hypermutation.
Evolution	Commonly used to refer to gradual change, evolution is the change in the frequency of alleles within a population from one generation to the next. This change may be caused by different mechanisms, including natural selection, genetic drift, or changes in population (gene flow).
Selective breeding	Selective breeding refers to the mating of those members of a strain of animals or plants that manifest a particular characteristic, which may or may not be done deliberately, to affect the genetic makeup of future generations of that strain.
Physiological psychology	Physiological psychology refers to the study of the physiological mechanisms, in the brain and elsewhere, that mediate behavior and psychological experiences.
Evolutionary psychology	Evolutionary psychology proposes that cognition and behavior can be better understood in light of evolutionary history.
Punishment	Punishment is the addtion of a stimulus that reduces the frequency of a response, or the removal of a stimulus that results in a reduction of the response.
Ego	In Freud's view the Ego serves to balance our primitive needs and our moral beliefs and taboos. Relying on experience, a healthy Ego provides the ability to adapt to reality and interact with the outside world.
Neurotic anxiety	Neurotic anxiety refers to, in psychoanalytic theory, a fear of the consequences of expressing previously punished and repressed id impulses; more generally, unrealistic fear.
Guilt	Guilt describes many concepts related to a negative emotion or condition caused by actions which are believed to be, morally wrong. According to Freud, the avoidance of guilt is the basis for moral behavior.
Insight	Insight refers to a sudden awareness of the relationships among various elements that had previously appeared to be independent of one another.
Acquisition	Acquisition is the process of adapting to the environment, learning or becoming conditioned. In classical conditoning terms, it is the initial learning of the stimulus response link, which involves a neutral stimulus being associated with a unconditioned stimulus and becoming a conditioned stimulus.
Relearning	Relearning refers to a measure of retention used in experiments on memory. Material is usually relearned more quickly than it is learned initially.
Fixed action pattern	A behavior that occurs in essentially identical fashion among most members of a species, that is elicited by a specific environmental stimulus, and is typically more complex than a reflex, is a fixed action pattern.
Emotion	An emotion is a mental states that arise spontaneously, rather than through conscious effort. They are often accompanied by physiological changes.
Elaboration	The extensiveness of processing at any given level of memory is called elaboration. The use of elaboration changes developmentally. Adolescents are more likely to use elaboration spontaneously than children.
Thematic Apperception Test	The Thematic Apperception Test uses a standard series of provocative yet ambiguous pictures about which the subject must tell a story. Each story is carefully analyzed to uncover underlying needs, attitudes, and patterns of reaction.
Apperception	A newly experienced sensation is related to past experiences to form an understood situation. For Wundt, consciousness is composed of two "stages:" There is a large capacity working memory called the Blickfeld and the narrower consciousness called Apperception, or selective attention.

Go to **Cram101.com** for the Practice Tests for this Chapter.

Chapter 1. Themes in the Study of Motivation

Projective test	A projective test is a personality test designed to let a person respond to ambiguous stimuli, presumably revealing hidden emotions and internal conflicts. This is different from an "objective test" in which responses are analyzed according to a universal standard rather than an individual psychiatrist's judgement.
Need for achievement	Need for Achievement is a term introduced by David McClelland into the field of psychology, referring to an individual's desire for significant accomplishment, mastering of skills, control, or high standards.
Need for Affiliation	Need for Affiliation is a term introduced by David McClelland to describe a person's need to feel like he needs to belong to a group. These individuals require warm interpersonal relationships and approval from those in these relationships is very satisfying. People who value affiliation a lot tend to be good team members, but poor leaders.
Need for Power	Need for Power is a term introduced by David McClelland referring to an individual's need to be in charge. There are two kinds of power, social and personal.
Self-actualization	Self-actualization (a term originated by Kurt Goldstein) is the instinctual need of a human to make the most of their unique abilities. Maslow described it as follows: Self Actualization is the intrinsic growth of what is already in the organism, or more accurately, of what the organism is.
Shaping	The concept of reinforcing successive, increasingly accurate approximations to a target behavior is called shaping. The target behavior is broken down into a hierarchy of elemental steps, each step more sophisticated then the last. By successively reinforcing each of the the elemental steps, a form of differential reinforcement, until that step is learned while extinguishing the step below, the target behavior is gradually achieved.
Achievement motive	The need to master difficult challenges, to outperform others, and to meet high standards of excellence is called the achievement motive.
Factor analysis	Factor analysis is a statistical technique that originated in psychometrics. The objective is to explain the most of the variability among a number of observable random variables in terms of a smaller number of unobservable random variables called factors.
Five-factor model	The five-factor model of personality proposes that there are five universal dimensions of personality: Neuroticism, Extraversion, Openness, Conscientiousness, and Agreeableness.
Personality test	A personality test aims to describe aspects of a person's character that remain stable across situations.
Personality trait	According to the Diagnostic and Statistical Manual of the American Psychiatric Association, a personality trait is a "prominent aspect of personality that is exhibited in a wide range of important social and personal contexts. ...".
Trait	An enduring personality characteristic that tends to lead to certain behaviors is called a trait. The term trait also means a genetically inherited feature of an organism.
Depression	In everyday language depression refers to any downturn in mood, which may be relatively transitory and perhaps due to something trivial. This is differentiated from Clinical depression which is marked by symptoms that last two weeks or more and are so severe that they interfere with daily living.
Attitude	An enduring mental representation of a person, place, or thing that evokes an emotional response and related behavior is called attitude.
Population	Population refers to all members of a well-defined group of organisms, events, or things.
Empirical	Empirical means the use of working hypotheses which are capable of being disproved using observation or experiment.
Growth needs	Maslow's hierarchy of needs is often depicted as a pyramid consisting of five levels: the four lower levels are grouped together as deficiency needs, while the top level is termed growth needs, those of

Chapter 1. Themes in the Study of Motivation

Chapter 1. Themes in the Study of Motivation

	self-actualization.
Behaviorism	The school of psychology that defines psychology as the study of observable behavior and studies relationships between stimuli and responses is called behaviorism. Behaviorism relied heavily on animal research and stated the same principles governed the behavior of both nonhumans and humans.
Modeling	A type of behavior learned through observation of others demonstrating the same behavior is modeling.
Classical conditioning	Classical conditioning is a simple form of learning in which an organism comes to associate or anticipate events. A neutral stimulus comes to evoke the response usually evoked by a natural or unconditioned stimulus by being paired repeatedly with the unconditioned stimulus.
Conditioning	Conditioning describes the process by which behaviors can be learned or modified through interaction with the environment.
Instrumental learning	Operant conditioning, sometimes called instrumental learning, was first extensively studied by Thorndike. In instrumental learning, the organism must act in a certain way before it is reinforced; that is, reinforcement is contingent on the organism's behavior.
Ejaculation	Ejaculation is the process of ejecting semen from the penis, and is usually accompanied by orgasm as a result of sexual stimulation.
Partial reinforcement	In a partial reinforcement environment, not every correct response is reinforced. Partial reinforcement is usually introduced after a continuous reinforcement schedule has acquired the behavior.
Reinforcement contingencies	The circumstances or rules that determine whether responses lead to the presentation of reinforcers are referred to as reinforcement contingencies. Skinner defined culture as a set of reinforcement contingencies.
Schedules of Reinforcement	Different combinations of frequency and timing of reinforcement following a behavior are referred to as schedules of reinforcement. They are either continuous (the behavior is reinforced each time it occurs) or intermittent (the behavior is reinforced only on certain occasions).
Behavior modification	Behavior Modification is a technique of altering an individual's reactions to stimuli through positive reinforcement and the extinction of maladaptive behavior.
Social learning	Social learning is learning that occurs as a function of observing, retaining and replicating behavior observed in others. Although social learning can occur at any stage in life, it is thought to be particularly important during childhood, particularly as authority becomes important.
Social learning theory	Social learning theory explains the process of gender typing in terms of observation, imitation, and role playing.
Adaptive behavior	An adaptive behavior increases the probability of the individual or organism to survive or exist within its environment.
Utopian	An ideal vision of society is a utopian society.
Stimulus	A change in an environmental condition that elicits a response is a stimulus.
Mental processes	The thoughts, feelings, and motives that each of us experiences privately but that cannot be observed directly are called mental processes.
Mastery orientation	According to Dweck, mastery orientation is an outlook in which individuals focus on the task rather than on their ability, have positive affect, and generate solution-oriented strategies that improve their performance.
Self-concept	Self-concept refers to domain-specific evaluations of the self where a domain may be academics, athletics, etc.
Perception	Perception is the process of acquiring, interpreting, selecting, and organizing sensory information.

Go to Cram101.com for the Practice Tests for this Chapter.

Chapter 1. Themes in the Study of Motivation

Resurgence	Resurgence refers to the reappearance during extinction, of a previously reinforced behavior.
Adaptation	Adaptation is a lowering of sensitivity to a stimulus following prolonged exposure to that stimulus. Behavioral adaptations are special ways a particular organism behaves to survive in its natural habitat.
Mental Representation	Stage six of the sensorimotor substages, Mental representation, 18 months to 2 years, marks the beginnings of insight, or true creativity. This marks the passage into unique thought in Piaget's later three areas of development.
Latent learning	The theory of latent learning describes learning that occurs in the absence of an obvious reward. Learning does not depend on reinforcement, but can go on in its absence and show up when reinforcement is introduced. Free exploration can be as effective as many previously reinforced trials according to Tolman.
Control group	A group that does not receive the treatment effect in an experiment is referred to as the control group or sometimes as the comparison group.
Variable	A variable refers to a measurable factor, characteristic, or attribute of an individual or a system.
Self-efficacy expectations	Beliefs to the effect that one can handle a task, that one can bring about desired changes through one's own efforts are called self-efficacy expectations.
Self-efficacy	Self-efficacy is the belief that one has the capabilities to execute the courses of actions required to manage prospective situations.
Bulimia	Bulimia refers to a disorder in which a person binges on incredibly large quantities of food, then purges by vomiting or by using laxatives. Bulimia is often less about food, and more to do with deep psychological issues and profound feelings of lack of control.
Binge	Binge refers to relatively brief episode of uncontrolled, excessive consumption.
Obsession	An obsession is a thought or idea that the sufferer cannot stop thinking about. Common examples include fears of acquiring disease, getting hurt, or causing harm to someone. They are typically automatic, frequent, distressing, and difficult to control or put an end to by themselves.
Self-esteem	Self-esteem refers to a person's subjective appraisal of himself or herself as intrinsically positive or negative to some degree.
Extraversion	Extraversion, one of the big-five personailty traits, is marked by pronounced engagement with the external world. They are people who enjoy being with people, are full of energy, and often experience positive emotions.
Neuroticism	Eysenck's use of the term neuroticism (or Emotional Stability) was proposed as the dimension describing individual differences in the predisposition towards neurotic disorder.
Agreeableness	Agreeableness, one of the big-five personality traits, reflects individual differences in concern with cooperation and social harmony. It is the degree individuals value getting along with others.
Conscientiouness	Conscientiousness is one of the dimensions of the five-factor model of personality and individual differences involving being organized, thorough, and reliable as opposed to careless, negligent, and unreliable.

Chapter 1. Themes in the Study of Motivation

Chapter 2. Components of Motivation

Motivation	In psychology, motivation is the driving force (desire) behind all actions of an organism.
Self-esteem	Self-esteem refers to a person's subjective appraisal of himself or herself as intrinsically positive or negative to some degree.
Brain circuits	Neurotransmitter currents or neural pathways in the brain are referred to as brain circuits.
Brain	The brain controls and coordinates most movement, behavior and homeostatic body functions such as heartbeat, blood pressure, fluid balance and body temperature. Functions of the brain are responsible for cognition, emotion, memory, motor learning and other sorts of learning. The brain is primarily made up of two types of cells: glia and neurons.
Evolutionary psychology	Evolutionary psychology proposes that cognition and behavior can be better understood in light of evolutionary history.
Evolution	Commonly used to refer to gradual change, evolution is the change in the frequency of alleles within a population from one generation to the next. This change may be caused by different mechanisms, including natural selection, genetic drift, or changes in population (gene flow).
Species	Species refers to a reproductively isolated breeding population.
Learning	Learning is a relatively permanent change in behavior that results from experience. Thus, to attribute a behavioral change to learning, the change must be relatively permanent and must result from experience.
Problem solving	An attempt to find an appropriate way of attaining a goal when the goal is not readily available is called problem solving.
Adaptation	Adaptation is a lowering of sensitivity to a stimulus following prolonged exposure to that stimulus. Behavioral adaptations are special ways a particular organism behaves to survive in its natural habitat.
Gene	A gene is an ultramicroscopic area of the chromosome. It is the smallest physical unit of the DNA molecule that carries a piece of hereditary information.
Sociobiology	Sociobiology is a synthesis of scientific disciplines that attempts to explain behavior in all species by considering the evolutionary advantages of social behaviors.
Predisposition	Predisposition refers to an inclination or diathesis to respond in a certain way, either inborn or acquired. In abnormal psychology, it is a factor that lowers the ability to withstand stress and inclines the individual toward pathology.
Temperament	Temperament refers to a basic, innate disposition to change behavior. The activity level is an important dimension of temperament.
Personality	Personality refers to the pattern of enduring characteristics that differentiates a person, the patterns of behaviors that make each individual unique.
Attention	Attention is the cognitive process of selectively concentrating on one thing while ignoring other things. Psychologists have labeled three types of attention: sustained attention, selective attention, and divided attention.
Extraversion	Extraversion, one of the big-five personailty traits, is marked by pronounced engagement with the external world. They are people who enjoy being with people, are full of energy, and often experience positive emotions.
Neuroticism	Eysenck's use of the term neuroticism (or Emotional Stability) was proposed as the dimension describing individual differences in the predisposition towards neurotic disorder.
Agreeableness	Agreeableness, one of the big-five personality traits, reflects individual differences in concern with cooperation and social harmony. It is the degree individuals value getting along with others.

Go to **Cram101.com** for the Practice Tests for this Chapter.

Chapter 2. Components of Motivation

Chapter 2. Components of Motivation

Conscientiousness	Conscientiousness is one of the dimensions of the five-factor model of personality and individual differences involving being organized, thorough, and reliable as opposed to careless, negligent, and unreliable.
Individual differences	Individual differences psychology studies the ways in which individual people differ in their behavior. This is distinguished from other aspects of psychology in that although psychology is ostensibly a study of individuals, modern psychologists invariably study groups.
Life span	Life span refers to the upper boundary of life, the maximum number of years an individual can live. The maximum life span of human beings is about 120 years of age. Females live an average of 6 years longer than males.
Variance	The degree to which scores differ among individuals in a distribution of scores is the variance.
Cognition	The intellectual processes through which information is obtained, transformed, stored, retrieved, and otherwise used is cognition.
Big five	The big five factors of personality are Openness to experience, Conscientiousness, Extraversion, Agreeableness, and Emotional Stability.
Correlation	A statistical technique for determining the degree of association between two or more variables is referred to as correlation.
Evolutionary perspective	A perspective that focuses on how humans have evolved and adapted behaviors required for survival against various environmental pressures over the long course is called the evolutionary perspective.
Monozygotic	Identical twins occur when a single egg is fertilized to form one zygote, calld monozygotic, but the zygote then divides into two separate embryos. The two embryos develop into foetuses sharing the same womb. Monozygotic twins are genetically identical unless there has been a mutation in development, and they are almost always the same gender.
Dizygotic	Fraternal twins (commonly known as "non-identical twins") usually occur when two fertilized eggs are implanted in the uterine wall at the same time. The two eggs form two zygotes, and these twins are therefore also known as dizygotic.
Chromosome	The DNA which carries genetic information in biological cells is normally packaged in the form of one or more large macromolecules called a chromosome. Humans normally have 46.
Socialization	Social rules and social relations are created, communicated, and changed in verbal and nonverbal ways creating social complexity useful in identifying outsiders and intelligent breeding partners. The process of learning these skills is called socialization.
Obesity	The state of being more than 20 percent above the average weight for a person of one's height is called obesity.
Variability	Statistically, variability refers to how much the scores in a distribution spread out, away from the mean.
Nerve	A nerve is an enclosed, cable-like bundle of nerve fibers or axons, which includes the glia that ensheath the axons in myelin. Neurons are sometimes called nerve cells, though this term is technically imprecise since many neurons do not form nerves.
Sensory receptor	A sensory receptor is a structure that recognizes a stimulus in the environment of an organism. In response to stimuli the sensory receptor initiates sensory transduction by creating graded potentials or action potentials in the same cell or in an adjacent one.
Receptor	A sensory receptor is a structure that recognizes a stimulus in the internal or external environment of an organism. In response to stimuli the sensory receptor initiates sensory transduction by creating graded potentials or action potentials in the same cell or in an

Chapter 2. Components of Motivation

Chapter 2. Components of Motivation

	adjacent one.
Emotion	An emotion is a mental states that arise spontaneously, rather than through conscious effort. They are often accompanied by physiological changes.
Variable	A variable refers to a measurable factor, characteristic, or attribute of an individual or a system.
Acquisition	Acquisition is the process of adapting to the environment, learning or becoming conditioned. In classical conditoning terms, it is the initial learning of the stimulus response link, which involves a neutral stimulus being associated with a unconditioned stimulus and becoming a conditioned stimulus.
Adaptive behavior	An adaptive behavior increases the probability of the individual or organism to survive or exist within its environment.
Depression	In everyday language depression refers to any downturn in mood, which may be relatively transitory and perhaps due to something trivial. This is differentiated from Clinical depression which is marked by symptoms that last two weeks or more and are so severe that they interfere with daily living.
Amphetamine	Amphetamine is a synthetic stimulant used to suppress the appetite, control weight, and treat disorders including narcolepsy and ADHD. It is also used recreationally and for performance enhancement.
Affect	A subjective feeling or emotional tone often accompanied by bodily expressions noticeable to others is called affect.
Reinforcement	In operant conditioning, reinforcement is any change in an environment that (a) occurs after the behavior, (b) seems to make that behavior re-occur more often in the future and (c) that reoccurence of behavior must be the result of the change.
Limbic system	The limbic system is a group of brain structures that are involved in various emotions such as aggression, fear, pleasure and also in the formation of memory. The limbic system affects the endocrine system and the autonomic nervous system. It consists of several subcortical structures located around the thalamus.
Reticular activating system	The reticular activating system is the part of the brain believed to be the center of arousal and motivation. It is situated between the brain stem and the central nervous system (CNS).
Synapse	A synapse is specialized junction through which cells of the nervous system signal to one another and to non-neuronal cells such as muscles or glands.
Neurotransmitter	A neurotransmitter is a chemical that is used to relay, amplify and modulate electrical signals between a neurons and another cell.
Serotonin	Serotonin, a neurotransmitter, is believed to play an important part of the biochemistry of depression, bipolar disorder and anxiety. It is also believed to be influential on sexuality and appetite.
Dopamine	Dopamine is critical to the way the brain controls our movements and is a crucial part of the basal ganglia motor loop. It is commonly associated with the 'pleasure system' of the brain, providing feelings of enjoyment and reinforcement to motivate us to do, or continue doing, certain activities.
Norepinephrine	Norepinephrine is released from the adrenal glands as a hormone into the blood, but it is also a neurotransmitter in the nervous system. As a stress hormone, it affects parts of the human brain where attention and impulsivity are controlled. Along with epinephrine, this compound effects the fight-or-flight response, activating the sympathetic nervous system to

Chapter 2. Components of Motivation

Chapter 2. Components of Motivation

	directly increase heart rate, release energy from fat, and increase muscle readiness.
Neuron	The neuron is the primary cell of the nervous system. They are found in the brain, the spinal cord, in the nerves and ganglia of the peripheral nervous system. It is a specialized cell that conducts impulses through the nervous system and contains three major parts: cell body, dendrites, and an axon. It can have many dendrites but only one axon.
Tricyclic antidepressant	A tricyclic antidepressant is of a class of antidepressant drugs first used in the 1950s. They are named after the drugs' molecular structure, which contains three rings of atoms.
Antidepressant	An antidepressant is a medication used primarily in the treatment of clinical depression. They are not thought to produce tolerance, although sudden withdrawal may produce adverse effects. They create little if any immediate change in mood and require between several days and several weeks to take effect.
Tricyclic	Tricyclic antidepressants are a class of antidepressant drugs first used in the 1950s. They are named after the drugs' molecular structure, which contains three rings of atoms.
Antidepressants	Antidepressants are medications used primarily in the treatment of clinical depression. Antidepressants create little if any immediate change in mood and require between several days and several weeks to take effect.
Cocaine	Cocaine is a crystalline tropane alkaloid that is obtained from the leaves of the coca plant. It is a stimulant of the central nervous system and an appetite suppressant, creating what has been described as a euphoric sense of happiness and increased energy.
Amino acid	Amino acid is the basic structural building unit of proteins. They form short polymer chains called peptides or polypeptides which in turn form structures called proteins.
Anxiety	Anxiety is a complex combination of the feeling of fear, apprehension and worry often accompanied by physical sensations such as palpitations, chest pain and/or shortness of breath.
Information processing	Information processing is an approach to the goal of understanding human thinking. The essence of the approach is to see cognition as being essentially computational in nature, with mind being the software and the brain being the hardware.
Endorphin	An endorphin is an endogenous opioid biochemical compound. They are peptides produced by the pituitary gland and the hypothalamus, and they resemble the opiates in their abilities to produce analgesia and a sense of well-being. In other words, they work as "natural pain killers."
Heroin	Heroin is widely and illegally used as a powerful and addictive drug producing intense euphoria, which often disappears with increasing tolerance. Heroin is a semi-synthetic opioid. It is the 3,6-diacetyl derivative of morphine and is synthesised from it by acetylation.
Morphine	Morphine, the principal active agent in opium, is a powerful opioid analgesic drug. According to recent research, it may also be produced naturally by the human brain. Morphine is usually highly addictive, and tolerance and physical and psychological dependence develop quickly.
Stress management	Stress management encompasses techniques intended to equip a person with effective coping mechanisms for dealing with psychological stress.
Feedback	Feedback refers to information returned to a person about the effects a response has had.
Selective attention	Selective attention is a type of attention which involves focusing on a specific aspect of a scene while ignoring other aspects.
Perception	Perception is the process of acquiring, interpreting, selecting, and organizing sensory information.

Chapter 2. Components of Motivation

Chapter 2. Components of Motivation

Associative learning	A metal connection made between two events is called associative learning.
Cognitive learning	Higher-level learning involving thinking, knowing, understanding, and anticipation is cognitive learning.
Construct	A generalized concept, such as anxiety or gravity, is a construct.
Attention deficit/hype-activity disorder	Disorders of childhood and adolescence characterized by socially disruptive behaviors-either attentional problems or hyperactivity-that persist for at least six months are an attention deficit/hyperactivity disorder.
Motivational processes	In observational learning, the motivational processes are the degree to which a behavior is seen to result in a valued outcome (expectancies) will influence the likelihood that one will adopt a modeled behavior.
Survey	A method of scientific investigation in which a large sample of people answer questions about their attitudes or behavior is referred to as a survey.
Theories	Theories are logically self-consistent models or frameworks describing the behavior of a certain natural or social phenomenon. They are broad explanations and predictions concerning phenomena of interest.
Conditioning	Conditioning describes the process by which behaviors can be learned or modified through interaction with the environment.
Classical conditioning	Classical conditioning is a simple form of learning in which an organism comes to associate or anticipate events. A neutral stimulus comes to evoke the response usually evoked by a natural or unconditioned stimulus by being paired repeatedly with the unconditioned stimulus.
Unconditioned stimulus	In classical conditioning, an unconditioned stimulus elicits a response from an organism prior to conditioning. It is a naturally occurring stimulus and a naturally occurring response..
Stimulus	A change in an environmental condition that elicits a response is a stimulus.
Unconditioned response	An Unconditioned Response is the response elicited to an unconditioned stimulus. It is a natural, automatic response.
Conditioned stimulus	A previously neutral stimulus that elicits the conditioned response because of being repeatedly paired with a stimulus that naturally elicited that response, is called a conditioned stimulus.
Conditioned response	A conditioned response is the response to a stimulus that occurs when an animal has learned to associate the stimulus with a certain positive or negative effect.
Extinction	In operant extinction, if no reinforcement is delivered after the response, gradually the behavior will no longer occur in the presence of the stimulus. The process is more rapid following continuous reinforcement rather than after partial reinforcement. In Classical Conditioning, repeated presentations of the CS without being followed by the US results in the extinction of the CS.
Blocking	If the one of the two members of a compound stimulus fails to produce the CR due to an earlier conditioning of the other member of the compound stimulus, blocking has occurred.
Addiction	Addiction is an uncontrollable compulsion to repeat a behavior regardless of its consequences. Many drugs or behaviors can precipitate a pattern of conditions recognized as addiction, which include a craving for more of the drug or behavior, increased physiological tolerance to exposure, and withdrawal symptoms in the absence of the stimulus.

Chapter 2. Components of Motivation

Chapter 2. Components of Motivation

Opponent process theory	The opponent process theory is a color theory that states that the human visual system interprets information about color by processing signals from cones in an antagonistic manner.
Instrumental learning	Operant conditioning, sometimes called instrumental learning, was first extensively studied by Thorndike. In instrumental learning, the organism must act in a certain way before it is reinforced; that is, reinforcement is contingent on the organism's behavior.
Partial reinforcement	In a partial reinforcement environment, not every correct response is reinforced. Partial reinforcement is usually introduced after a continuous reinforcement schedule has acquired the behavior.
Reinforcer	In operant conditioning, a reinforcer is any stimulus that increases the probability that a preceding behavior will occur again. In Classical Conditioning, the unconditioned stimulus (US) is the reinforcer.
Incentive	An incentive is what is expected once a behavior is performed. An incentive acts as a reinforcer.
Punishment	Punishment is the addtion of a stimulus that reduces the frequency of a response, or the removal of a stimulus that results in a reduction of the response.
Empirical	Empirical means the use of working hypotheses which are capable of being disproved using observation or experiment.
Incentive value	The value of a goal above and beyond its ability to fill a need is its incentive value.
Pavlovian conditioning	Pavlovian conditioning, synonymous with classical conditioning is a type of learning found in animals, caused by the association (or pairing) of two stimuli or what Ivan Pavlov described as the learning of conditional behavior, therefore called conditioning.
Fear response	In the Mowrer-Miller theory, a response to a threatening or noxious situation that is covert but that is assumed to function as a stimulus to produce measurable physiological changes in the body and observable overt behavior is referred to as the fear response.
Amygdala	Located in the brain's medial temporal lobe, the almond-shaped amygdala is believed to play a key role in the emotions. It forms part of the limbic system and is linked to both fear responses and pleasure. Its size is positively correlated with aggressive behavior across species.
Associative process	The process that connects two stimuli, a stimulus and a response, or a response and a reinforcer is an associative process.
Secondary Reinforcer	A conditioned reinforcer, sometimes called a secondary reinforcer, is a stimulus or situation that has acquired reinforcing power after being paired in the environment with an unconditioned reinforcer or an earlier conditioned reinforcer.
Schemata	Cognitive categories or frames of reference are called schemata.
Assimilation	According to Piaget, assimilation is the process of the organism interacting with the environment given the organism's cognitive structure. Assimilation is reuse of schemas to fit new information.
Accommodation	Piaget's developmental process of accommodation is the modification of currently held schemes or new schemes so that new information inconsistent with the existing schemes can be integrated and understood.
Attitude	An enduring mental representation of a person, place, or thing that evokes an emotional response and related behavior is called attitude.
Modeling	A type of behavior learned through observation of others demonstrating the same behavior is

Chapter 2. Components of Motivation

	modeling.
Alcoholic	An alcoholic is dependent on alcohol as characterized by craving, loss of control, physical dependence and withdrawal symptoms, and tolerance.
Cognitive psychology	Cognitive psychology is the psychological science which studies the mental processes that are hypothesised to underlie behavior. This covers a broad range of research domains, examining questions about the workings of memory, attention, perception, knowledge representation, reasoning, creativity and problem solving.
Habit	A habit is a response that has become completely separated from its eliciting stimulus. Early learning theorists used the term to describe S-R associations, however not all S-R associations become a habit, rather many are extinguished after reinforcement is withdrawn.
Generalization	In conditioning, the tendency for a conditioned response to be evoked by stimuli that are similar to the stimulus to which the response was conditioned is a generalization. The greater the similarity among the stimuli, the greater the probability of generalization.
Stereotype	A stereotype is considered to be a group concept, held by one social group about another. They are often used in a negative or prejudicial sense and are frequently used to justify certain discriminatory behaviors. This allows powerful social groups to legitimize and protect their dominant position
Piaget's theory	Piaget's theory describes children actively constructing their understanding of the world, passing through four stages of cognitive development. The dual mechanisms of assimilation and accomodation, along with the driving force of equilibration, provide for slow but steady intellectual growth.
Cognitive development	The process by which a child's understanding of the world changes as a function of age and experience is called cognitive development.
Cognitive dissonance	Cognitive dissonance is a state of opposition between cognitions. Contradicting cognitions serve as a driving force that compel the mind to acquire or invent new thoughts or beliefs, or to modify existing beliefs, so as to minimize the amount of dissonance between cognitions.
Reasoning	Reasoning is the act of using reason to derive a conclusion from certain premises. There are two main methods to reach a conclusion, deductive reasoning and inductive reasoning.
Preconscious	In psychodynamic theory, material that is not in awareness but that can be brought into awareness by focusing one's attention is referred to as preconscious.
Nervous system	The body's electrochemical communication circuitry, made up of billions of neurons is a nervous system.
Chronic	Chronic refers to a relatively long duration, usually more than a few months.
Achievement motivation	The psychological need in humans for success is called achievement motivation.
Placebo	Placebo refers to a bogus treatment that has the appearance of being genuine.
Locus of control	The place to which an individual attributes control over the receiving of reinforcers -either inside or outside the self is referred to as locus of control.
Causation	Causation concerns the time order relationship between two or more objects such that if a specific antecendent condition occurs the same consequent must always follow.
Forethought	Forethought is a person's capability to motivate themselves and guide their actions anticipatorily. Stimuli are not automatically linked to the response by contiguity. Instead, previous experiences create expectations of the outcome that will occur as a result of performing a behavior, before the behavior is performed.

Chapter 2. Components of Motivation

Chapter 2. Components of Motivation

Attribution theory	Attribution theory is concerned with the ways in which people explain the behavior of others. It explores how individuals "attribute" causes to events and how this cognitive perception affects their motivation.
Attribution process	The process by which people draw inferences about the motives and traits of others is the attribution process.
Compulsion	An apparently irresistible urge to repeat an act or engage in ritualistic behavior such as hand washing is referred to as a compulsion.
Aerobic exercise	Aerobic exercise is a type of exercise in which muscles draw on oxygen in the blood as well as fats and glucose, that increase cardiovascular endurance.
Immune response	The body's defensive reaction to invasion by bacteria, viral agents, or other foreign substances is called the immune response.
Epinephrine	Epinephrine is a hormone and a neurotransmitter. Epinephrine plays a central role in the short-term stress reaction—the physiological response to threatening or exciting conditions. It is secreted by the adrenal medulla. When released into the bloodstream, epinephrine binds to multiple receptors and has numerous effects throughout the body.
Scientific research	Research that is objective, systematic, and testable is called scientific research.
Knowledge base	The general background information a person possesses, which influences most cognitive task performance is called the knowledge base.
Enzyme	An enzyme is a protein that catalyzes, or speeds up, a chemical reaction. Enzymes are essential to sustain life because most chemical reactions in biological cells would occur too slowly, or would lead to different products, without enzymes.
Monoamine oxidase	Monoamine oxidase is an enzyme that catalyzes the oxidation of monoamines. They are found bound to the outer membrane of mitochondria in most cell types in the body. Because of the vital role that it play in the inactivation of neurotransmitters, dysfunction (too much/too little MAO activity) is thought to be responsible for a number of neurological disorders.
Motives	Needs or desires that energize and direct behavior toward a goal are motives.

Chapter 2. Components of Motivation

Chapter 3. Hunger and Eating

Hormone	A hormone is a chemical messenger from one cell (or group of cells) to another. The best known are those produced by endocrine glands, but they are produced by nearly every organ system. The function of hormones is to serve as a signal to the target cells; the action of the hormone is determined by the pattern of secretion and the signal transduction of the receiving tissue.
Neurotransmitter	A neurotransmitter is a chemical that is used to relay, amplify and modulate electrical signals between a neurons and another cell.
Obesity	The state of being more than 20 percent above the average weight for a person of one's height is called obesity.
Evolutionary perspective	A perspective that focuses on how humans have evolved and adapted behaviors required for survival against various environmental pressures over the long course is called the evolutionary perspective.
Gene	A gene is an ultramicroscopic area of the chromosome. It is the smallest physical unit of the DNA molecule that carries a piece of hereditary information.
Conditioning	Conditioning describes the process by which behaviors can be learned or modified through interaction with the environment.
Fetus	A fetus develops from the end of the 8th week of pregnancy (when the major structures have formed), until birth.
Hypothesis	A specific statement about behavior or mental processes that is testable through research is a hypothesis.
Spontaneous abortion	Spontaneous abortion is the natural or accidental termination of a pregnancy at a stage where the embryo or the fetus is incapable of surviving, generally defined at a gestation less than 20 weeks.
Species	Species refers to a reproductively isolated breeding population.
Stimulus	A change in an environmental condition that elicits a response is a stimulus.
Learning	Learning is a relatively permanent change in behavior that results from experience. Thus, to attribute a behavioral change to learning, the change must be relatively permanent and must result from experience.
Evolution	Commonly used to refer to gradual change, evolution is the change in the frequency of alleles within a population from one generation to the next. This change may be caused by different mechanisms, including natural selection, genetic drift, or changes in population (gene flow).
Attention	Attention is the cognitive process of selectively concentrating on one thing while ignoring other things. Psychologists have labeled three types of attention: sustained attention, selective attention, and divided attention.
Embryo	A developed zygote that has a rudimentary heart, brain, and other organs is referred to as an embryo.
Glucose	Glucose, a simple monosaccharide sugar, is one of the most important carbohydrates and is used as a source of energy in animals and plants. Glucose is one of the main products of photosynthesis and starts respiration.
Metabolism	Metabolism is the biochemical modification of chemical compounds in living organisms and cells.
Brain	The brain controls and coordinates most movement, behavior and homeostatic body functions such as heartbeat, blood pressure, fluid balance and body temperature. Functions of the brain are responsible for cognition, emotion, memory, motor learning and other sorts of learning.

Go to Cram101.com for the Practice Tests for this Chapter.

Chapter 3. Hunger and Eating

Chapter 3. Hunger and Eating

	The brain is primarily made up of two types of cells: glia and neurons.
Amino acid	Amino acid is the basic structural building unit of proteins. They form short polymer chains called peptides or polypeptides which in turn form structures called proteins.
Thiamine	Thiamine, also known as vitamin B1, is a colorless compound with chemical formula $C_{12}H_{17}ClN_4OS$. Systemic thiamine deficiency can lead to myriad problems including neurodegeneration, wasting, and death. Well-known syndromes caused by lack of thiamine due to malnutrition or a diet high in thiaminase-rich foods include Wernicke-Korsakoff syndrome and beriberi, diseases also common in chronic abusers of alcohol.
Norepinephrine	Norepinephrine is released from the adrenal glands as a hormone into the blood, but it is also a neurotransmitter in the nervous system. As a stress hormone, it affects parts of the human brain where attention and impulsivity are controlled. Along with epinephrine, this compound effects the fight-or-flight response, activating the sympathetic nervous system to directly increase heart rate, release energy from fat, and increase muscle readiness.
Serotonin	Serotonin, a neurotransmitter, is believed to play an important part of the biochemistry of depression, bipolar disorder and anxiety. It is also believed to be influential on sexuality and appetite.
Ethnic group	An ethnic group is a culture or subculture whose members are readily distinguishable by outsiders based on traits originating from a common racial, national, linguistic, or religious source. Members of an ethnic group are often presumed to be culturally or biologically similar, although this is not in fact necessarily the case.
Stages	Stages represent relatively discrete periods of time in which functioning is qualitatively different from functioning at other periods.
Modeling	A type of behavior learned through observation of others demonstrating the same behavior is modeling.
Deprivation	Deprivation, is the loss or withholding of normal stimulation, nutrition, comfort, love, and so forth; a condition of lacking. The level of stimulation is less than what is required.
Scientific research	Research that is objective, systematic, and testable is called scientific research.
Coronary heart disease	Coronary heart disease is the end result of the accumulation of atheromatous plaques within the walls of the arteries that supply the myocardium (the muscle of the heart).
Satiety	Satiety refers to the state of being satisfied; fullness.
Chronic	Chronic refers to a relatively long duration, usually more than a few months.
Fraternal twins	Fraternal twins usually occur when two fertilized eggs are implanted in the uterine wall at the same time. The two eggs form two zygotes, and these twins are therefore also known as dizygotic. Dizygotic twins are no more similar genetically than any siblings.
Identical twins	Identical twins occur when a single egg is fertilized to form one zygote (monozygotic) but the zygote then divides into two separate embryos. The two embryos develop into foetuses sharing the same womb. Monozygotic twins are genetically identical unless there has been a mutation in development, and they are almost always the same gender.
Metabolic rate	Metabolic rate refers to the rate at which the body burns calories to produce energy.
Individual differences	Individual differences psychology studies the ways in which individual people differ in their behavior. This is distinguished from other aspects of psychology in that although psychology is ostensibly a study of individuals, modern psychologists invariably study groups.
Hypothalamus	The hypothalamus is a region of the brain located below the thalamus, forming the major

Chapter 3. Hunger and Eating

	portion of the ventral region of the diencephalon and functioning to regulate certain metabolic processes and other autonomic activities.
Leptin	Leptin refers to a hormone produced by fat cells that acts in the brain to inhibit hunger and regulate body weight.
Receptor	A sensory receptor is a structure that recognizes a stimulus in the internal or external environment of an organism. In response to stimuli the sensory receptor initiates sensory transduction by creating graded potentials or action potentials in the same cell or in an adjacent one.
Lesion	A lesion is a non-specific term referring to abnormal tissue in the body. It can be caused by any disease process including trauma (physical, chemical, electrical), infection, neoplasm, metabolic and autoimmune.
Bulimia	Bulimia refers to a disorder in which a person binges on incredibly large quantities of food, then purges by vomiting or by using laxatives. Bulimia is often less about food, and more to do with deep psychological issues and profound feelings of lack of control.
Eating disorders	Psychological disorders characterized by distortion of the body image and gross disturbances in eating patterns are called eating disorders.
Set point	Set point refers to any one of a number of quantities (e.g. body weight, body temperature) which the body tries to keep at a particular value
Construct	A generalized concept, such as anxiety or gravity, is a construct.
Habit	A habit is a response that has become completely separated from its eliciting stimulus. Early learning theorists used the term to describe S-R associations, however not all S-R associations become a habit, rather many are extinguished after reinforcement is withdrawn.
Depression	In everyday language depression refers to any downturn in mood, which may be relatively transitory and perhaps due to something trivial. This is differentiated from Clinical depression which is marked by symptoms that last two weeks or more and are so severe that they interfere with daily living.
Antecedents	In behavior modification, events that typically precede the target response are called antecedents.
Prospective study	Prospective study is a long-term study of a group of people, beginning before the onset of a common disorder. It allows investigators to see how the disorder develops.
Motivation	In psychology, motivation is the driving force (desire) behind all actions of an organism.
Theories	Theories are logically self-consistent models or frameworks describing the behavior of a certain natural or social phenomenon. They are broad explanations and predictions concerning phenomena of interest.
Motility	Motility is the ability to move spontaneously and independently. The term can apply to single cells, or to multicellular organisms.
Gland	A gland is an organ in an animal's body that synthesizes a substance for release such as hormones, often into the bloodstream or into cavities inside the body or its outer surface.
Galvanic skin response	Galvanic skin response is a method of measuring the electrical resistance of the skin and interpreting it as an image of activity in certain parts of the body.
Baseline	Measure of a particular behavior or process taken before the introduction of the independent variable or treatment is called the baseline.
Questionnaire	A self-report method of data collection or clinical assessment method in which the individual being studied checks off items on a printed list, answers multiple-choice questions, or

Chapter 3. Hunger and Eating

Chapter 3. Hunger and Eating

	writes out answers to essay questions aimed at producing a selfdescription is called questionnaire.
Control subjects	Control subjects are participants in an experiment who do not receive the treatment effect but for whom all other conditions are held comparable to those of experimental subjects.
Perception	Perception is the process of acquiring, interpreting, selecting, and organizing sensory information.
Affect	A subjective feeling or emotional tone often accompanied by bodily expressions noticeable to others is called affect.
Attitude	An enduring mental representation of a person, place, or thing that evokes an emotional response and related behavior is called attitude.
Disinhibition	A temporary increase in the strength of an extinguished response caused by an unrelated stimulus event is referred to as disinhibition.
Norms	In testing, standards of test performance that permit the comparison of one person's score on the test to the scores of others who have taken the same test are referred to as norms.
Obsession	An obsession is a thought or idea that the sufferer cannot stop thinking about. Common examples include fears of acquiring disease, getting hurt, or causing harm to someone. They are typically automatic, frequent, distressing, and difficult to control or put an end to by themselves.
Behavior modification	Behavior Modification is a technique of altering an individual's reactions to stimuli through positive reinforcement and the extinction of maladaptive behavior.
Autonomy	Autonomy is the condition of something that does not depend on anything else.
Hypertension	Hypertension is a medical condition where the blood pressure in the arteries is chronically elevated. Persistent hypertension is one of the risk factors for strokes, heart attacks, heart failure and arterial aneurysm, and is a leading cause of chronic renal failure.
Cardiovascular disease	Cardiovascular disease refers to afflictions in the mechanisms, including the heart, blood vessels, and their controllers, that are responsible for transporting blood to the body's tissues and organs. Psychological factors may play important roles in such diseases and their treatments.
Variability	Statistically, variability refers to how much the scores in a distribution spread out, away from the mean.
Adaptation	Adaptation is a lowering of sensitivity to a stimulus following prolonged exposure to that stimulus. Behavioral adaptations are special ways a particular organism behaves to survive in its natural habitat.
Altruism	Altruism is being helpful to other people with little or no interest in being rewarded for one's efforts. This is distinct from merely helping others.
Empathy	Empathy is the recognition and understanding of the states of mind, including beliefs, desires and particularly emotions of others without injecting your own.
Problem solving	An attempt to find an appropriate way of attaining a goal when the goal is not readily available is called problem solving.

Chapter 3. Hunger and Eating

Chapter 4. Passion, Love, and Sexual Behavior

Stereotype	A stereotype is considered to be a group concept, held by one social group about another. They are often used in a negative or prejudicial sense and are frequently used to justify certain discriminatory behaviors. This allows powerful social groups to legitimize and protect their dominant position
Physiology	The study of the functions and activities of living cells, tissues, and organs and of the physical and chemical phenomena involved is referred to as physiology.
Hormone	A hormone is a chemical messenger from one cell (or group of cells) to another. The best known are those produced by endocrine glands, but they are produced by nearly every organ system. The function of hormones is to serve as a signal to the target cells; the action of the hormone is determined by the pattern of secretion and the signal transduction of the receiving tissue.
Sexual orientation	Sexual orientation refers to the sex or gender of people who are the focus of a person's amorous or erotic desires, fantasies, and spontaneous feelings, the gender(s) toward which one is primarily "oriented".
Motivation	In psychology, motivation is the driving force (desire) behind all actions of an organism.
Stages	Stages represent relatively discrete periods of time in which functioning is qualitatively different from functioning at other periods.
Tactile	Pertaining to the sense of touch is referred to as tactile.
Paradigm	Paradigm refers to the set of practices that defines a scientific discipline during a particular period of time. It provides a framework from which to conduct research, it ensures that a certain range of phenomena, those on which the paradigm focuses, are explored thoroughly. It may also blind scientists to other, perhaps more fruitful, ways of dealing with their subject matter.
Sensation	Sensation is the first stage in the chain of biochemical and neurologic events that begins with the impinging of a stimulus upon the receptor cells of a sensory organ, which then leads to perception, the mental state that is reflected in statements like "I see a uniformly blue wall."
Excitement phase	The excitement phase refers to the first phase of the sexual response cycle, characterized by muscle tension, increases in the heart rate, and erection in the male and vaginal lubrication in the female.
Plateau phase	The plateau phase is the second phase of the sexual cycle. Further increases in circulation and heart rate occur in both sexes, sexual pleasure increases with increased stimulation, muscle tension increases further.
Resolution phase	The resolution phase refers to the fourth phase of the sexual response cycle. The resolution phase occurs after orgasm and allows the muscles to relax, blood pressure to drop and the body to slow down from its excited state.
Physiological changes	Alterations in heart rate, blood pressure, perspiration, and other involuntary responses are physiological changes.
Clitoris	Clitoris refers to an external female sex organ that is highly sensitive to sexual stimulation.
Receptor	A sensory receptor is a structure that recognizes a stimulus in the internal or external environment of an organism. In response to stimuli the sensory receptor initiates sensory transduction by creating graded potentials or action potentials in the same cell or in an adjacent one.
Vasocongestion	Engorgement of blood vessels with blood, which swells the genitals and breasts during sexual

Go to Cram101.com for the Practice Tests for this Chapter.

Chapter 4. Passion, Love, and Sexual Behavior

Chapter 4. Passion, Love, and Sexual Behavior

	arousal is called vasocongestion.
Ejaculation	Ejaculation is the process of ejecting semen from the penis, and is usually accompanied by orgasm as a result of sexual stimulation.
Stimulus	A change in an environmental condition that elicits a response is a stimulus.
Script	A schema, or behavioral sequence, for an event is called a script. It is a form of schematic organization, with real-world events organized in terms of temporal and causal relations between component acts.
Schemata	Cognitive categories or frames of reference are called schemata.
Sexual script	A sexual script is a stereotyped pattern of role prescriptions for how individuals should behave sexually.
Motives	Needs or desires that energize and direct behavior toward a goal are motives.
Punishment	Punishment is the addtion of a stimulus that reduces the frequency of a response, or the removal of a stimulus that results in a reduction of the response.
Modeling	A type of behavior learned through observation of others demonstrating the same behavior is modeling.
Adolescence	The period of life bounded by puberty and the assumption of adult responsibilities is adolescence.
Masturbation	Masturbation is the manual excitation of the sexual organs, most often to the point of orgasm. It can refer to excitation either by oneself or by another, but commonly refers to such activities performed alone.
Gender role	A cluster of behaviors that characterizes traditional female or male behaviors within a cultural setting is a gender role.
Learning	Learning is a relatively permanent change in behavior that results from experience. Thus, to attribute a behavioral change to learning, the change must be relatively permanent and must result from experience.
Attention	Attention is the cognitive process of selectively concentrating on one thing while ignoring other things. Psychologists have labeled three types of attention: sustained attention, selective attention, and divided attention.
Generalization	In conditioning, the tendency for a conditioned response to be evoked by stimuli that are similar to the stimulus to which the response was conditioned is a generalization. The greater the similarity among the stimuli, the greater the probability of generalization.
Variable	A variable refers to a measurable factor, characteristic, or attribute of an individual or a system.
Attitude	An enduring mental representation of a person, place, or thing that evokes an emotional response and related behavior is called attitude.
Sexually Transmitted Disease	Sexually transmitted disease is commonly transmitted between partners through some form of sexual activity, most commonly vaginal intercourse, oral sex, or anal sex.
Mental Representation	Stage six of the sensorimotor substages, Mental representation, 18 months to 2 years, marks the beginnings of insight, or true creativity. This marks the passage into unique thought in Piaget's later three areas of development.
Individual differences	Individual differences psychology studies the ways in which individual people differ in their behavior. This is distinguished from other aspects of psychology in that although psychology

Chapter 4. Passion, Love, and Sexual Behavior

Chapter 4. Passion, Love, and Sexual Behavior

	is ostensibly a study of individuals, modern psychologists invariably study groups.
Evolutionary perspective	A perspective that focuses on how humans have evolved and adapted behaviors required for survival against various environmental pressures over the long course is called the evolutionary perspective.
Gene	A gene is an ultramicroscopic area of the chromosome. It is the smallest physical unit of the DNA molecule that carries a piece of hereditary information.
Evolution	Commonly used to refer to gradual change, evolution is the change in the frequency of alleles within a population from one generation to the next. This change may be caused by different mechanisms, including natural selection, genetic drift, or changes in population (gene flow).
Brain	The brain controls and coordinates most movement, behavior and homeostatic body functions such as heartbeat, blood pressure, fluid balance and body temperature. Functions of the brain are responsible for cognition, emotion, memory, motor learning and other sorts of learning. The brain is primarily made up of two types of cells: glia and neurons.
Species	Species refers to a reproductively isolated breeding population.
Dopamine	Dopamine is critical to the way the brain controls our movements and is a crucial part of the basal ganglia motor loop. It is commonly associated with the 'pleasure system' of the brain, providing feelings of enjoyment and reinforcement to motivate us to do, or continue doing, certain activities.
Norepinephrine	Norepinephrine is released from the adrenal glands as a hormone into the blood, but it is also a neurotransmitter in the nervous system. As a stress hormone, it affects parts of the human brain where attention and impulsivity are controlled. Along with epinephrine, this compound effects the fight-or-flight response, activating the sympathetic nervous system to directly increase heart rate, release energy from fat, and increase muscle readiness.
Attachment	Attachment is the tendency to seek closeness to another person and feel secure when that person is present.
Endorphin	An endorphin is an endogenous opioid biochemical compound. They are peptides produced by the pituitary gland and the hypothalamus, and they resemble the opiates in their abilities to produce analgesia and a sense of well-being. In other words, they work as "natural pain killers."
Morphine	Morphine, the principal active agent in opium, is a powerful opioid analgesic drug. According to recent research, it may also be produced naturally by the human brain. Morphine is usually highly addictive, and tolerance and physical and psychological dependence develop quickly.
Emotion	An emotion is a mental states that arise spontaneously, rather than through conscious effort. They are often accompanied by physiological changes.
Immune system	The most important function of the human immune system occurs at the cellular level of the blood and tissues. The lymphatic and blood circulation systems are highways for specialized white blood cells. These cells include B cells, T cells, natural killer cells, and macrophages. All function with the primary objective of recognizing, attacking and destroying bacteria, viruses, cancer cells, and all substances seen as foreign.
Nerve	A nerve is an enclosed, cable-like bundle of nerve fibers or axons, which includes the glia that ensheath the axons in myelin. Neurons are sometimes called nerve cells, though this term is technically imprecise since many neurons do not form nerves.
Oxytocin	Oxytocin is synthesized in magnocellular neurosecretory cells in the hypothalamus and released by the posterior lobe of the pituitary gland. It is involved in the facilitation of birth and breastfeeding as well as in bonding.

Chapter 4. Passion, Love, and Sexual Behavior

Trait	An enduring personality characteristic that tends to lead to certain behaviors is called a trait. The term trait also means a genetically inherited feature of an organism.
Theories	Theories are logically self-consistent models or frameworks describing the behavior of a certain natural or social phenomenon. They are broad explanations and predictions concerning phenomena of interest.
Evolutionary psychology	Evolutionary psychology proposes that cognition and behavior can be better understood in light of evolutionary history.
Self-concept	Self-concept refers to domain-specific evaluations of the self where a domain may be academics, athletics, etc.
Self-esteem	Self-esteem refers to a person's subjective appraisal of himself or herself as intrinsically positive or negative to some degree.
Self-efficacy	Self-efficacy is the belief that one has the capabilities to execute the courses of actions required to manage prospective situations.
Connectedness	Connectedness, according to Cooper, consists of two dimensions: mutuality and permeability. Connectedness involves processes that link the self to others, as seen in acknowledgment of, respect for, and responsiveness to others.
Self-disclosure	The process of revealing private thoughts, feelings, and one's personal history to others is referred to as self-disclosure.
Personality type	A persistent style of complex behaviors defined by a group of related traits is referred to as a personality type. Myer Friedman and his co-workers first defined personality types in the 1950s. Friedman classified people into 2 categories, Type A and Type B.
Personality	Personality refers to the pattern of enduring characteristics that differentiates a person, the patterns of behaviors that make each individual unique.
Cognition	The intellectual processes through which information is obtained, transformed, stored, retrieved, and otherwise used is cognition.
Schema	Schema refers to a way of mentally representing the world, such as a belief or an expectation, that can influence perception of persons, objects, and situations.
Friendship	The essentials of friendship are reciprocity and commitment between individuals who see themselves more or less as equals. Interaction between friends rests on a more equal power base than the interaction between children and adults.
Romantic love	An intense, positive emotion that involves sexual attraction, feelings of caring, and the belief that one is in love is romantic love.
Companionate love	Companionate love is a form of love that combines friendship and commitment. Companionate love is generally a personal relation you build with somebody you share your life with, but with no sexual or physical desire.
Consummate love	Consummate love is the most complete type of love experienced in interpersonal relationships, the three major components: intimacy, passion and commitment, are all present and balanced.
Y chromosome	The Y chromosome is one of the two sex chromosomes in humans and most other mammals. The sex chromosomes are one of the 23 pairs of human chromosomes. The Y chromosome contains the fewest genes of any of the chromosomes. It contains the genes that cause testis development, thus determining maleness. It is usually contributed by the father.
Chromosome	The DNA which carries genetic information in biological cells is normally packaged in the form of one or more large macromolecules called a chromosome. Humans normally have 46.
Fetus	A fetus develops from the end of the 8th week of pregnancy (when the major structures have

Chapter 4. Passion, Love, and Sexual Behavior

Chapter 4. Passion, Love, and Sexual Behavior

	formed), until birth.
Infancy	The developmental period that extends from birth to 18 or 24 months is called infancy.
Androgen	Androgen is the generic term for any natural or synthetic compound, usually a steroid hormone, that stimulates or controls the development and maintenance of masculine characteristics in vertebrates by binding to androgen receptors.
Testosterone	Testosterone is a steroid hormone from the androgen group. It is the principal male sex hormone and the "original" anabolic steroid.
Estrogen	Estrogen is a group of steroid compounds that function as the primary female sex hormone. They are produced primarily by developing follicles in the ovaries, the corpus luteum and the placenta.
Progestin	A hormone used to maintain pregnancy that can cause masculinization of the fetus is progestin.
Estradiol	Estradiol is a sex hormone. Labelled the "female" hormone but also present in males it represents the major estrogen in humans. Critical for sexual functioning estradiol also supports bone growth.
Progesterone	A female sex hormone that promotes growth of the sex organs and helps maintain pregnancy is called progesterone.
Adrenal glands	The adrenal glands sit atop the kidneys. They are chiefly responsible for regulating the stress response through the synthesis of corticosteroids and catecholamines, including cortisol and adrenalin.
Gland	A gland is an organ in an animal's body that synthesizes a substance for release such as hormones, often into the bloodstream or into cavities inside the body or its outer surface.
Gonads	The gonads are the organs that make gametes. Gametes are haploid germ cells. For example, sperm and egg cells are gametes. In the male the gonads are the testicles, and in the female the gonads are the ovaries.
Testes	Testes are the male reproductive glands or gonads; this is where sperm develop and are stored.
Pituitary gland	The pituitary gland is an endocrine gland about the size of a pea that sits in the small, bony cavity at the base of the brain. The pituitary gland secretes hormones regulating a wide variety of bodily activities, including trophic hormones that stimulate other endocrine glands.
Hypothalamus	The hypothalamus is a region of the brain located below the thalamus, forming the major portion of the ventral region of the diencephalon and functioning to regulate certain metabolic processes and other autonomic activities.
Ovulation	Ovulation is the process in the menstrual cycle by which a mature ovarian follicle ruptures and discharges an ovum (also known as an oocyte, female gamete, or casually, an egg) that participates in reproduction.
Self-fulfilling prophecy	A self-fulfilling prophecy is a prediction that, in being made, actually causes itself to become true.
Ovum	Ovum is a female sex cell or gamete.
Ovary	The female reproductive organ is the ovary. It performs two major functions: producing eggs and secreting hormones.
Menopause	Menopause is a stage of the human female reproductive cycle that occurs as the ovaries stop producing estrogen, causing the reproductive system to gradually shut down.

Chapter 4. Passion, Love, and Sexual Behavior

Chapter 4. Passion, Love, and Sexual Behavior

X chromosome	The sex chromosomes are one of the 23 pairs of human chromosomes. Each person normally has one pair of sex chromosomes in each cell. Females have two X chromosomes, while males have one X and one Y chromosome. The X chromosome carries hundreds of genes but few, if any, of these have anything to do directly with sex determination.
Antigen	An antigen is a molecule that stimulates the production of antibodies. Usually, it is a protein or a polysaccharide, but can be any type of molecule, including small molecules (haptens) coupled to a protein (carrier).
Transsexual	A transsexual person establishes a permanent identity with the opposite gender to their assigned sex. They make or desire to make a transition from their birth sex to that of the opposite sex, with some type of medical alteration to their body.
Mental rotation	The ability to change the position of an image in mental space is called mental rotation.
Standard deviation	In probability and statistics, the standard deviation is the most commonly used measure of statistical dispersion. Simply put, it measures how spread out the values in a data set are.
Effect size	An effect size is the strength or magnitude of the difference between two sets of data or, in outcome studies, between two time points for the same population. (The degree to which the null hypothesis is false).
Puberty	Puberty refers to the process of physical changes by which a child's body becomes an adult body capable of reproduction.
Reasoning	Reasoning is the act of using reason to derive a conclusion from certain premises. There are two main methods to reach a conclusion, deductive reasoning and inductive reasoning.
Meta-analysis	In statistics, a meta-analysis combines the results of several studies that address a set of related research hypotheses.
Population	Population refers to all members of a well-defined group of organisms, events, or things.
Prenatal	Prenatal period refers to the time from conception to birth.
Neuron	The neuron is the primary cell of the nervous system. They are found in the brain, the spinal cord, in the nerves and ganglia of the peripheral nervous system. It is a specialized cell that conducts impulses through the nervous system and contains three major parts: cell body, dendrites, and an axon. It can have many dendrites but only one axon.
Nucleus	In neuroanatomy, a cluster of cell bodies of neurons within the central nervous system is a nucleus.
Cerebral cortex	The cerebral cortex is the outermost layer of the cerebrum and has a grey color. It is made up of four lobes and it is involved in many complex brain functions including memory, perceptual awareness, "thinking", language and consciousness. The cerebral cortex receives sensory information from many different sensory organs eg: eyes, ears, etc. and processes the information.
Right hemisphere	The brain is divided into left and right cerebral hemispheres. The right hemisphere of the cortex controls the left side of the body.
Corpus callosum	The corpus callosum is the largest white matter structure in the brain. It consists of mostly of contralateral axon projections. The corpus callosum connects the left and right cerebral hemispheres. Most communication between regions in different halves of the brain are carried over the corpus callosum.
Lateralization	Lateralization refers to the dominance of one hemisphere of the brain for specific functions.
Amygdala	Located in the brain's medial temporal lobe, the almond-shaped amygdala is believed to play a key role in the emotions. It forms part of the limbic system and is linked to both fear

Chapter 4. Passion, Love, and Sexual Behavior

	responses and pleasure. Its size is positively correlated with aggressive behavior across species.
Critical period	A period of time when an innate response can be elicited by a particular stimulus is referred to as the critical period.
Gender identity	Gender identity describes the gender with which a person identifies, but can also be used to refer to the gender that other people attribute to the individual on the basis of what they know from gender role indications.
Homosexuality	Homosexuality refers to a sexual orientation characterized by aesthetic attraction, romantic love, and sexual desire exclusively for members of the same sex or gender identity.
Homosexual	Homosexual refers to a sexual orientation characterized by aesthetic attraction, romantic love, and sexual desire exclusively for members of the same sex or gender identity.
Heritability	Heritability It is that proportion of the observed variation in a particular phenotype within a particular population, that can be attributed to the contribution of genotype. In other words: it measures the extent to which differences between individuals in a population are due their being different genetically.
Identical twins	Identical twins occur when a single egg is fertilized to form one zygote (monozygotic) but the zygote then divides into two separate embryos. The two embryos develop into foetuses sharing the same womb. Monozygotic twins are genetically identical unless there has been a mutation in development, and they are almost always the same gender.
Fraternal twins	Fraternal twins usually occur when two fertilized eggs are implanted in the uterine wall at the same time. The two eggs form two zygotes, and these twins are therefore also known as dizygotic. Dizygotic twins are no more similar genetically than any siblings.
Genetics	Genetics is the science of genes, heredity, and the variation of organisms.
Lesbian	A lesbian is a homosexual woman. They are women who are sexually and romantically attracted to other women.
Castration	Castration is any action, surgical, chemical or otherwise, by which a biological male loses use of the testes. This causes sterilization, i.e. prevents him from reproducing; it also greatly reduces the production of certain hormones, such as testosterone.
Affect	A subjective feeling or emotional tone often accompanied by bodily expressions noticeable to others is called affect.
Congenital	A condition existing at birth is referred to as congenital.
Control group	A group that does not receive the treatment effect in an experiment is referred to as the control group or sometimes as the comparison group.
Hypothesis	A specific statement about behavior or mental processes that is testable through research is a hypothesis.
Pathology	Pathology is the study of the processes underlying disease and other forms of illness, harmful abnormality, or dysfunction.
Psychoanalytic theory	Psychoanalytic theory is a general term for approaches to psychoanalysis which attempt to provide a conceptual framework more-or-less independent of clinical practice rather than based on empirical analysis of clinical cases.
Psychoanalytic	Freud's theory that unconscious forces act as determinants of personality is called psychoanalytic theory. The theory is a developmental theory characterized by critical stages of development.
Role model	A person who serves as a positive example of desirable behavior is referred to as a role

Chapter 4. Passion, Love, and Sexual Behavior

	model.
Enzyme	An enzyme is a protein that catalyzes, or speeds up, a chemical reaction. Enzymes are essential to sustain life because most chemical reactions in biological cells would occur too slowly, or would lead to different products, without enzymes.
Variance	The degree to which scores differ among individuals in a distribution of scores is the variance.
Heredity	Heredity is the transfer of characteristics from parent to offspring through their genes.
Anxiety	Anxiety is a complex combination of the feeling of fear, apprehension and worry often accompanied by physical sensations such as palpitations, chest pain and/or shortness of breath.
Depression	In everyday language depression refers to any downturn in mood, which may be relatively transitory and perhaps due to something trivial. This is differentiated from Clinical depression which is marked by symptoms that last two weeks or more and are so severe that they interfere with daily living.
Suicidal ideation	Suicidal ideation refers to having serious thoughts about committing suicide.
Gender schema	Gender schema refers to a cognitive structure that organizes the world in terms of maleness and femaleness.
Homophobia	An intense, irrational hostility toward or fear of homosexuals is referred to as homophobia.
Heterosexuality	Sexual attraction and behavior directed to the opposite sex is heterosexuality.
Self-image	A person's self-image is the mental picture, generally of a kind that is quite resistant to change, that depicts not only details that are potentially available to objective investigation by others, but also items that have been learned by that person about himself or herself.
Plasticity	The capacity for modification and change is referred to as plasticity.
Discrimination	In Learning theory, discrimination refers the ability to distinguish between a conditioned stimulus and other stimuli. It can be brought about by extensive training or differential reinforcement. In social terms, it is the denial of privileges to a person or a group on the basis of prejudice.

Chapter 4. Passion, Love, and Sexual Behavior

Chapter 5. Arousal, Attention, and Peak Performance

Attention	Attention is the cognitive process of selectively concentrating on one thing while ignoring other things. Psychologists have labeled three types of attention: sustained attention, selective attention, and divided attention.
Brain	The brain controls and coordinates most movement, behavior and homeostatic body functions such as heartbeat, blood pressure, fluid balance and body temperature. Functions of the brain are responsible for cognition, emotion, memory, motor learning and other sorts of learning. The brain is primarily made up of two types of cells: glia and neurons.
Adaptive behavior	An adaptive behavior increases the probability of the individual or organism to survive or exist within its environment.
Information processing	Information processing is an approach to the goal of understanding human thinking. The essence of the approach is to see cognition as being essentially computational in nature, with mind being the software and the brain being the hardware.
Autonomic nervous system	A division of the peripheral nervous system, the autonomic nervous system, regulates glands and activities such as heartbeat, respiration, digestion, and dilation of the pupils. It is responsible for homeostasis, maintaining a relatively constant internal environment.
Nervous system	The body's electrochemical communication circuitry, made up of billions of neurons is a nervous system.
Reticular activating system	The reticular activating system is the part of the brain believed to be the center of arousal and motivation. It is situated between the brain stem and the central nervous system (CNS).
Sensory receptor	A sensory receptor is a structure that recognizes a stimulus in the environment of an organism. In response to stimuli the sensory receptor initiates sensory transduction by creating graded potentials or action potentials in the same cell or in an adjacent one.
Receptor	A sensory receptor is a structure that recognizes a stimulus in the internal or external environment of an organism. In response to stimuli the sensory receptor initiates sensory transduction by creating graded potentials or action potentials in the same cell or in an adjacent one.
Tactile	Pertaining to the sense of touch is referred to as tactile.
Nerve	A nerve is an enclosed, cable-like bundle of nerve fibers or axons, which includes the glia that ensheath the axons in myelin. Neurons are sometimes called nerve cells, though this term is technically imprecise since many neurons do not form nerves.
Projection	Attributing one's own undesirable thoughts, impulses, traits, or behaviors to others is referred to as projection.
Reticular formation	Reticular formation is a part of the brain which is involved in stereotypical actions, such as walking, sleeping, and lying down. The reticular formation, phylogenetically one of the oldest portions of the brain, is a poorly-differentiated area of the brain stem.
Electrode	Any device used to electrically stimulate nerve tissue or to record its activity is an electrode.
Schemata	Cognitive categories or frames of reference are called schemata.
Motor cortex	Motor cortex refers to the section of cortex that lies in the frontal lobe, just across the central fissure from the sensory cortex. Neural impulses in the motor cortex are linked to muscular responses throughout the body.
Amplitude	Amplitude is a nonnegative scalar measure of a wave's magnitude of oscillation.
Positron	Positron Emission Tomography measures emissions from radioactively labeled chemicals that

Chapter 5. Arousal, Attention, and Peak Performance

emission tomography	have been injected into the bloodstream. The greatest benefit is that different compounds can show blood flow and oxygen and glucose metabolism in the tissues of the working brain.
Epilepsy	Epilepsy is a chronic neurological condition characterized by recurrent unprovoked neural discharges. It is commonly controlled with medication, although surgical methods are used as well.
Emotion	An emotion is a mental states that arise spontaneously, rather than through conscious effort. They are often accompanied by physiological changes.
Physiological changes	Alterations in heart rate, blood pressure, perspiration, and other involuntary responses are physiological changes.
Stimulus	A change in an environmental condition that elicits a response is a stimulus.
Anxiety	Anxiety is a complex combination of the feeling of fear, apprehension and worry often accompanied by physical sensations such as palpitations, chest pain and/or shortness of breath.
Glucose	Glucose, a simple monosaccharide sugar, is one of the most important carbohydrates and is used as a source of energy in animals and plants. Glucose is one of the main products of photosynthesis and starts respiration.
Hypothalamus	The hypothalamus is a region of the brain located below the thalamus, forming the major portion of the ventral region of the diencephalon and functioning to regulate certain metabolic processes and other autonomic activities.
Sympathetic	The sympathetic nervous system activates what is often termed the "fight or flight response". It is an automatic regulation system, that is, one that operates without the intervention of conscious thought.
Adrenal medulla	Composed mainly of hormone-producing chromaffin cells, the adrenal medulla is the principal site of the conversion of the amino acid tyrosine into the catecholamines epinephrine and norepinephrine (also called adrenaline and noradrenaline, respectively).
Epinephrine	Epinephrine is a hormone and a neurotransmitter. Epinephrine plays a central role in the short-term stress reaction—the physiological response to threatening or exciting conditions. It is secreted by the adrenal medulla. When released into the bloodstream, epinephrine binds to multiple receptors and has numerous effects throughout the body.
Norepinephrine	Norepinephrine is released from the adrenal glands as a hormone into the blood, but it is also a neurotransmitter in the nervous system. As a stress hormone, it affects parts of the human brain where attention and impulsivity are controlled. Along with epinephrine, this compound effects the fight-or-flight response, activating the sympathetic nervous system to directly increase heart rate, release energy from fat, and increase muscle readiness.
Affect	A subjective feeling or emotional tone often accompanied by bodily expressions noticeable to others is called affect.
Motivation	In psychology, motivation is the driving force (desire) behind all actions of an organism.
Baseline	Measure of a particular behavior or process taken before the introduction of the independent variable or treatment is called the baseline.
Problem solving	An attempt to find an appropriate way of attaining a goal when the goal is not readily available is called problem solving.
Yerkes-Dodson law	The Yerkes-Dodson law shows an empirical relationship between arousal and performance. Performance increases with cognitive arousal but only to a certain point: when levels of arousal become too high, performance will decrease. A corollary is that there is an optimal level of arousal for a given task.

Chapter 5. Arousal, Attention, and Peak Performance

Sensory deprivation	Sensory deprivation is the deliberate reduction or removal of stimuli from one or more of the senses. Though short periods of sensory deprivation can be relaxing, extended deprivation can result in extreme anxiety, hallucinations, bizarre thoughts, depression, and antisocial behavior.
Deprivation	Deprivation, is the loss or withholding of normal stimulation, nutrition, comfort, love, and so forth; a condition of lacking. The level of stimulation is less than what is required.
Hallucination	A hallucination is a sensory perception experienced in the absence of an external stimulus, as distinct from an illusion, which is a misperception of an external stimulus. They may occur in any sensory modality - visual, auditory, olfactory, gustatory, tactile, or mixed.
Learning	Learning is a relatively permanent change in behavior that results from experience. Thus, to attribute a behavioral change to learning, the change must be relatively permanent and must result from experience.
Need for achievement	Need for Achievement is a term introduced by David McClelland into the field of psychology, referring to an individual's desire for significant accomplishment, mastering of skills, control, or high standards.
Selective attention	Selective attention is a type of attention which involves focusing on a specific aspect of a scene while ignoring other aspects.
Limited capacity	Limited capacity refers to the concept that one's information processing ability is restricted. Metaphors for capacity include mental space, mental energy or effort, and time.
Evolutionary perspective	A perspective that focuses on how humans have evolved and adapted behaviors required for survival against various environmental pressures over the long course is called the evolutionary perspective.
Punishment	Punishment is the addtion of a stimulus that reduces the frequency of a response, or the removal of a stimulus that results in a reduction of the response.
Species	Species refers to a reproductively isolated breeding population.
Theories	Theories are logically self-consistent models or frameworks describing the behavior of a certain natural or social phenomenon. They are broad explanations and predictions concerning phenomena of interest.
Pituitary gland	The pituitary gland is an endocrine gland about the size of a pea that sits in the small, bony cavity at the base of the brain. The pituitary gland secretes hormones regulating a wide variety of bodily activities, including trophic hormones that stimulate other endocrine glands.
Gland	A gland is an organ in an animal's body that synthesizes a substance for release such as hormones, often into the bloodstream or into cavities inside the body or its outer surface.
Adrenal glands	The adrenal glands sit atop the kidneys. They are chiefly responsible for regulating the stress response through the synthesis of corticosteroids and catecholamines, including cortisol and adrenalin.
Arousal theory	Hebb proposed that attention was a function of arousal, the first arousal theory. Hebb proposed that all human beings have a need to maintain their arousal levels and that there is an optimal level for performance.
Variable	A variable refers to a measurable factor, characteristic, or attribute of an individual or a system.
Trait	An enduring personality characteristic that tends to lead to certain behaviors is called a trait. The term trait also means a genetically inherited feature of an organism.

Chapter 5. Arousal, Attention, and Peak Performance

Chapter 5. Arousal, Attention, and Peak Performance

Personality trait	According to the Diagnostic and Statistical Manual of the American Psychiatric Association, a personality trait is a "prominent aspect of personality that is exhibited in a wide range of important social and personal contexts. ...".
Personality	Personality refers to the pattern of enduring characteristics that differentiates a person, the patterns of behaviors that make each individual unique.
Cognitive dissonance	Cognitive dissonance is a state of opposition between cognitions. Contradicting cognitions serve as a driving force that compel the mind to acquire or invent new thoughts or beliefs, or to modify existing beliefs, so as to minimize the amount of dissonance between cognitions.
Test anxiety	High levels of arousal and worry that seriously impair test performance is referred to as test anxiety.
Self-image	A person's self-image is the mental picture, generally of a kind that is quite resistant to change, that depicts not only details that are potentially available to objective investigation by others, but also items that have been learned by that person about himself or herself.
Antecedents	In behavior modification, events that typically precede the target response are called antecedents.
Neuroticism	Eysenck's use of the term neuroticism (or Emotional Stability) was proposed as the dimension describing individual differences in the predisposition towards neurotic disorder.
Meditation	Meditation usually refers to a state in which the body is consciously relaxed and the mind is allowed to become calm and focused.
Population	Population refers to all members of a well-defined group of organisms, events, or things.
Phobia	A persistent, irrational fear of an object, situation, or activity that the person feels compelled to avoid is referred to as a phobia.
Concordance	Concordance as used in genetics means the presence of the same trait in both members of a pair of twins, or in sets of individuals. A twin study examines the concordance rates of twins having the same trait, especially a disease, which can help determine how much the disease is affected by genetics versus environment.
Monozygotic	Identical twins occur when a single egg is fertilized to form one zygote, calld monozygotic, but the zygote then divides into two separate embryos. The two embryos develop into foetuses sharing the same womb. Monozygotic twins are genetically identical unless there has been a mutation in development, and they are almost always the same gender.
Dizygotic	Fraternal twins (commonly known as "non-identical twins") usually occur when two fertilized eggs are implanted in the uterine wall at the same time. The two eggs form two zygotes, and these twins are therefore also known as dizygotic.
Physiology	The study of the functions and activities of living cells, tissues, and organs and of the physical and chemical phenomena involved is referred to as physiology.
Amygdala	Located in the brain's medial temporal lobe, the almond-shaped amygdala is believed to play a key role in the emotions. It forms part of the limbic system and is linked to both fear responses and pleasure. Its size is positively correlated with aggressive behavior across species.
Cognition	The intellectual processes through which information is obtained, transformed, stored, retrieved, and otherwise used is cognition.
Introvert	Introvert refers to a person whose attention is focused inward; a shy, reserved, timid person.

Chapter 5. Arousal, Attention, and Peak Performance

Socialization	Social rules and social relations are created, communicated, and changed in verbal and nonverbal ways creating social complexity useful in identifying outsiders and intelligent breeding partners. The process of learning these skills is called socialization.
Limbic system	The limbic system is a group of brain structures that are involved in various emotions such as aggression, fear, pleasure and also in the formation of memory. The limbic system affects the endocrine system and the autonomic nervous system. It consists of several subcortical structures located around the thalamus.
Extraversion	Extraversion, one of the big-five personailty traits, is marked by pronounced engagement with the external world. They are people who enjoy being with people, are full of energy, and often experience positive emotions.
Behavioral therapy	The treatment of a mental disorder through the application of basic principles of conditioning and learning is called behavioral therapy.
Behavioral inhibition system	The behavioral inhibition system is a circuit in the limbic system that responds to threat signals by inhibiting activity and causing anxiety.
Behavioral inhibition	Physiological probes of children with behavioral inhibition show significantly higher measures of activity in the sympathetic nervous system and hypothalamic-pituitary axis than in non-inhibited children. Kagan postulates that anxiety-prone children are born with a lower firing threshold in amygdala and hypothalamic neurons. His work provides a robust model for predicting temperamental forerunners of anxiety disorders.
Introversion	A personality trait characterized by intense imagination and a tendency to inhibit impulses is called introversion.
Preparedness	The species-specific biological predisposition to learn in certain ways is called preparedness.
Schema	Schema refers to a way of mentally representing the world, such as a belief or an expectation, that can influence perception of persons, objects, and situations.
Negative schema	Negative schema are automatic, enduring, and stable negative cognitive biases.
Depression	In everyday language depression refers to any downturn in mood, which may be relatively transitory and perhaps due to something trivial. This is differentiated from Clinical depression which is marked by symptoms that last two weeks or more and are so severe that they interfere with daily living.
Social learning	Social learning is learning that occurs as a function of observing, retaining and replicating behavior observed in others. Although social learning can occur at any stage in life, it is thought to be particularly important during childhood, particularly as authority becomes important.
Modeling	A type of behavior learned through observation of others demonstrating the same behavior is modeling.
Subjective experience	Subjective experience refers to reality as it is perceived and interpreted, not as it exists objectively.
Mental processes	The thoughts, feelings, and motives that each of us experiences privately but that cannot be observed directly are called mental processes.
Perception	Perception is the process of acquiring, interpreting, selecting, and organizing sensory information.
Necessary condition	A circumstance required for a particular phenomenon to occur is a necessary condition if and only if the condition does not occur in the absense of the circumstance.

Chapter 5. Arousal, Attention, and Peak Performance

Biological rhythm	A biological rhythm is a hypothetical cyclic pattern of alterations in physiology, emotions, and/or intellect
Neurotransmitter	A neurotransmitter is a chemical that is used to relay, amplify and modulate electrical signals between a neurons and another cell.
Serotonin	Serotonin, a neurotransmitter, is believed to play an important part of the biochemistry of depression, bipolar disorder and anxiety. It is also believed to be influential on sexuality and appetite.
Locus coeruleus	The Locus coeruleus is a nucleus in the brain stem (inferior to the cerebellum in the caudal midbrain/rostral pons) apparently responsible for the physiological reactions involved in stress and panic.
Biofeedback	Biofeedback is the process of measuring and quantifying an aspect of a subject's physiology, analyzing the data, and then feeding back the information to the subject in a form that allows the subject to enact physiological change.
Chronic	Chronic refers to a relatively long duration, usually more than a few months.
Psychological disorder	Mental processes and/or behavior patterns that cause emotional distress and/or substantial impairment in functioning is a psychological disorder.
Essential hypertension	Essential hypertension refers to a psychophysiological disorder characterized by high blood pressure that cannot be traced to an organic cause.
Hypertension	Hypertension is a medical condition where the blood pressure in the arteries is chronically elevated. Persistent hypertension is one of the risk factors for strokes, heart attacks, heart failure and arterial aneurysm, and is a leading cause of chronic renal failure.
Diastolic blood pressure	Blood pressure level when the heart is at rest or between heartbeats is called diastolic blood pressure.
Motivational state	A motivational state is an internal, reversible condition in an individual that orients the individual toward one or another type of goal. This condition is not observed directly but is inferred from the individual's behavior.
Attitude	An enduring mental representation of a person, place, or thing that evokes an emotional response and related behavior is called attitude.
Galvanic skin response	Galvanic skin response is a method of measuring the electrical resistance of the skin and interpreting it as an image of activity in certain parts of the body.
Hypothesis	A specific statement about behavior or mental processes that is testable through research is a hypothesis.
Immune system	The most important function of the human immune system occurs at the cellular level of the blood and tissues. The lymphatic and blood circulation systems are highways for specialized white blood cells. These cells include B cells, T cells, natural killer cells, and macrophages. All function with the primary objective of recognizing, attacking and destroying bacteria, viruses, cancer cells, and all substances seen as foreign.
Individual differences	Individual differences psychology studies the ways in which individual people differ in their behavior. This is distinguished from other aspects of psychology in that although psychology is ostensibly a study of individuals, modern psychologists invariably study groups.
Emotion-focused coping	Lazarus' emotion-focused coping describes individuals' response to stress demonstrated in an emotional manner, especially using defensive methods.
Median	The median is a number that separates the higher half of a sample, a population, or a probability distribution from the lower half. It is the middle value in a distribution, above

Chapter 5. Arousal, Attention, and Peak Performance

	and below which lie an equal number of values.
Human nature	Human nature is the fundamental nature and substance of humans, as well as the range of human behavior that is believed to be invariant over long periods of time and across very different cultural contexts.
Questionnaire	A self-report method of data collection or clinical assessment method in which the individual being studied checks off items on a printed list, answers multiple-choice questions, or writes out answers to essay questions aimed at producing a selfdescription is called questionnaire.
Mastery orientation	According to Dweck, mastery orientation is an outlook in which individuals focus on the task rather than on their ability, have positive affect, and generate solution-oriented strategies that improve their performance.
Social support	Social Support is the physical and emotional comfort given by family, friends, co-workers and others. Research has identified three main types of social support: emotional, practical, sharing points of view.
Denial	Denial is a psychological defense mechanism in which a person faced with a fact that is uncomfortable or painful to accept rejects it instead, insisting that it is not true despite what may be overwhelming evidence.
Self-esteem	Self-esteem refers to a person's subjective appraisal of himself or herself as intrinsically positive or negative to some degree.
Ego	In Freud's view the Ego serves to balance our primitive needs and our moral beliefs and taboos. Relying on experience, a healthy Ego provides the ability to adapt to reality and interact with the outside world.
Factor analysis	Factor analysis is a statistical technique that originated in psychometrics. The objective is to explain the most of the variability among a number of observable random variables in terms of a smaller number of unobservable random variables called factors.
Feedback	Feedback refers to information returned to a person about the effects a response has had.

Chapter 5. Arousal, Attention, and Peak Performance

Chapter 6. Wakefulness, Alertness, Sleep, and Dreams

Sleep patterns	The order and timing of daily sleep and waking periods are called sleep patterns.
Consciousness	The awareness of the sensations, thoughts, and feelings being experienced at a given moment is called consciousness.
Immune system	The most important function of the human immune system occurs at the cellular level of the blood and tissues. The lymphatic and blood circulation systems are highways for specialized white blood cells. These cells include B cells, T cells, natural killer cells, and macrophages. All function with the primary objective of recognizing, attacking and destroying bacteria, viruses, cancer cells, and all substances seen as foreign.
Metabolic rate	Metabolic rate refers to the rate at which the body burns calories to produce energy.
Testosterone	Testosterone is a steroid hormone from the androgen group. It is the principal male sex hormone and the "original" anabolic steroid.
Glucose	Glucose, a simple monosaccharide sugar, is one of the most important carbohydrates and is used as a source of energy in animals and plants. Glucose is one of the main products of photosynthesis and starts respiration.
Attention	Attention is the cognitive process of selectively concentrating on one thing while ignoring other things. Psychologists have labeled three types of attention: sustained attention, selective attention, and divided attention.
Information processing	Information processing is an approach to the goal of understanding human thinking. The essence of the approach is to see cognition as being essentially computational in nature, with mind being the software and the brain being the hardware.
Problem solving	An attempt to find an appropriate way of attaining a goal when the goal is not readily available is called problem solving.
Creativity	Creativity is the ability to think about something in novel and unusual ways and come up with unique solutions to problems. It involves divergent thinking, having many solutions or views to a problem.
Adaptation	Adaptation is a lowering of sensitivity to a stimulus following prolonged exposure to that stimulus. Behavioral adaptations are special ways a particular organism behaves to survive in its natural habitat.
Natural selection	Natural selection is a process by which biological populations are altered over time, as a result of the propagation of heritable traits that affect the capacity of individual organisms to survive and reproduce.
Evolution	Commonly used to refer to gradual change, evolution is the change in the frequency of alleles within a population from one generation to the next. This change may be caused by different mechanisms, including natural selection, genetic drift, or changes in population (gene flow).
Brain	The brain controls and coordinates most movement, behavior and homeostatic body functions such as heartbeat, blood pressure, fluid balance and body temperature. Functions of the brain are responsible for cognition, emotion, memory, motor learning and other sorts of learning. The brain is primarily made up of two types of cells: glia and neurons.
Species	Species refers to a reproductively isolated breeding population.
Stages	Stages represent relatively discrete periods of time in which functioning is qualitatively different from functioning at other periods.
Rapid eye movement	Rapid eye movement is the stage of sleep during which the most vivid (though not all) dreams occur. During this stage, the eyes move rapidly, and the activity of the brain's neurons is quite similar to that during waking hours. It is the lightest form of sleep in that people awakened during REM usually feel alert and refreshed.

Go to **Cram101.com** for the Practice Tests for this Chapter.

Chapter 6. Wakefulness, Alertness, Sleep, and Dreams

Chapter 6. Wakefulness, Alertness, Sleep, and Dreams

Rem sleep	Sleep characterized by rapid eye movements, paralysis of large muscles, fast and irregular heart rate and respiration rate, increased brain-wave activity, and vivid dreams is referred to as REM sleep. An infant spends about half the time in REM sleep when sleeping.
Metabolism	Metabolism is the biochemical modification of chemical compounds in living organisms and cells.
Nerve	A nerve is an enclosed, cable-like bundle of nerve fibers or axons, which includes the glia that ensheath the axons in myelin. Neurons are sometimes called nerve cells, though this term is technically imprecise since many neurons do not form nerves.
Reticular activating system	The reticular activating system is the part of the brain believed to be the center of arousal and motivation. It is situated between the brain stem and the central nervous system (CNS).
Serotonin	Serotonin, a neurotransmitter, is believed to play an important part of the biochemistry of depression, bipolar disorder and anxiety. It is also believed to be influential on sexuality and appetite.
Locus coeruleus	The Locus coeruleus is a nucleus in the brain stem (inferior to the cerebellum in the caudal midbrain/rostral pons) apparently responsible for the physiological reactions involved in stress and panic.
Norepinephrine	Norepinephrine is released from the adrenal glands as a hormone into the blood, but it is also a neurotransmitter in the nervous system. As a stress hormone, it affects parts of the human brain where attention and impulsivity are controlled. Along with epinephrine, this compound effects the fight-or-flight response, activating the sympathetic nervous system to directly increase heart rate, release energy from fat, and increase muscle readiness.
Light sleep	Stage 1 sleep, marked by small irregular brain waves and some alpha waves, is called light sleep.
Mental processes	The thoughts, feelings, and motives that each of us experiences privately but that cannot be observed directly are called mental processes.
Cerebral cortex	The cerebral cortex is the outermost layer of the cerebrum and has a grey color. It is made up of four lobes and it is involved in many complex brain functions including memory, perceptual awareness, "thinking", language and consciousness. The cerebral cortex receives sensory information from many different sensory organs eg: eyes, ears, etc. and processes the information.
Motor cortex	Motor cortex refers to the section of cortex that lies in the frontal lobe, just across the central fissure from the sensory cortex. Neural impulses in the motor cortex are linked to muscular responses throughout the body.
Emotion	An emotion is a mental states that arise spontaneously, rather than through conscious effort. They are often accompanied by physiological changes.
Circadian rhythm	The circadian rhythm is a name given to the "internal body clock" that regulates the (roughly) 24 hour cycle of biological processes in animals and plants.
Biological rhythm	A biological rhythm is a hypothetical cyclic pattern of alterations in physiology, emotions, and/or intellect
Chronic	Chronic refers to a relatively long duration, usually more than a few months.
Deprivation	Deprivation, is the loss or withholding of normal stimulation, nutrition, comfort, love, and so forth; a condition of lacking. The level of stimulation is less than what is required.
Epinephrine	Epinephrine is a hormone and a neurotransmitter. Epinephrine plays a central role in the short-term stress reaction—the physiological response to threatening or exciting conditions.

Chapter 6. Wakefulness, Alertness, Sleep, and Dreams

Chapter 6. Wakefulness, Alertness, Sleep, and Dreams

	It is secreted by the adrenal medulla. When released into the bloodstream, epinephrine binds to multiple receptors and has numerous effects throughout the body.
Adrenaline	Adrenaline refers to a hormone produced by the adrenal medulla that stimulates sympathetic ANS activity and generally arouses people and heightens their emotional responsiveness.
Adrenal glands	The adrenal glands sit atop the kidneys. They are chiefly responsible for regulating the stress response through the synthesis of corticosteroids and catecholamines, including cortisol and adrenalin.
Gland	A gland is an organ in an animal's body that synthesizes a substance for release such as hormones, often into the bloodstream or into cavities inside the body or its outer surface.
Hypothalamus	The hypothalamus is a region of the brain located below the thalamus, forming the major portion of the ventral region of the diencephalon and functioning to regulate certain metabolic processes and other autonomic activities.
Stimulant	A stimulant is a drug which increases the activity of the sympathetic nervous system and produces a sense of euphoria or awakeness.
Variable	A variable refers to a measurable factor, characteristic, or attribute of an individual or a system.
Extraversion	Extraversion, one of the big-five personailty traits, is marked by pronounced engagement with the external world. They are people who enjoy being with people, are full of energy, and often experience positive emotions.
Introversion	A personality trait characterized by intense imagination and a tendency to inhibit impulses is called introversion.
Personality	Personality refers to the pattern of enduring characteristics that differentiates a person, the patterns of behaviors that make each individual unique.
Slow-wave sleep	Slow-wave sleep includes stages 3 and 4, during which low-frequency delta waves become prominent in EEG recordings.
Affect	A subjective feeling or emotional tone often accompanied by bodily expressions noticeable to others is called affect.
Right hemisphere	The brain is divided into left and right cerebral hemispheres. The right hemisphere of the cortex controls the left side of the body.
Intuitive thought	Thinking that makes little or no use of reasoning and logic is referred to as intuitive thought.
Left hemisphere	The left hemisphere of the cortex controls the right side of the body, coordinates complex movements, and, in 95% of people, controls the production of speech and written language.
Stage 4 sleep	The deepest stage of sleep, during which we are least responsive to outside stimulation is referred to as stage 4 sleep.
Stage 2 sleep	A sleep deeper than that of stage 1, characterized by a slower, more regular wave pattern, along with momentary interruptions of 'sleep spindles' is called stage 2 sleep.
Primary drive	A primary drive is a state of tension or arousal arising from a biological or innate need; it is one not based on learning. A primary drive activates behavior.
Motivation	In psychology, motivation is the driving force (desire) behind all actions of an organism.
Immune response	The body's defensive reaction to invasion by bacteria, viral agents, or other foreign substances is called the immune response.
Microsleep	A microsleep is a period of sleep lasting a few seconds. It often occurs as a result of a

Chapter 6. Wakefulness, Alertness, Sleep, and Dreams

Chapter 6. Wakefulness, Alertness, Sleep, and Dreams

	sleep debt or mental fatigue.
Habituation	In habituation there is a progressive reduction in the response probability with continued repetition of a stimulus.
Feedback	Feedback refers to information returned to a person about the effects a response has had.
Parietal lobe	The parietal lobe is positioned above (superior to) the occipital lobe and behind (posterior to) the frontal lobe. It plays important roles in integrating sensory information from various senses, and in the manipulation of objects.
Lobes	The four major sections of the cerebral cortex: frontal, parietal, temporal, and occipital are called lobes.
Control group	A group that does not receive the treatment effect in an experiment is referred to as the control group or sometimes as the comparison group.
Sleep apnea	Sleep apnea refers to a sleep disorder involving periods during sleep when breathing stops and the person must awaken briefly in order to breathe; major symptoms are excessive daytime sleepiness and loud snoring.
Apnea	Apnea is the absence of external breathing. During apnea there is no movement of the muscles of respiration and the volume of the lungs initially remains unchanged. .
Antidepressant	An antidepressant is a medication used primarily in the treatment of clinical depression. They are not thought to produce tolerance, although sudden withdrawal may produce adverse effects. They create little if any immediate change in mood and require between several days and several weeks to take effect.
Depression	In everyday language depression refers to any downturn in mood, which may be relatively transitory and perhaps due to something trivial. This is differentiated from Clinical depression which is marked by symptoms that last two weeks or more and are so severe that they interfere with daily living.
Central nervous system	The vertebrate central nervous system consists of the brain and spinal cord.
Nervous system	The body's electrochemical communication circuitry, made up of billions of neurons is a nervous system.
Spinal cord	The spinal cord is a part of the vertebrate nervous system that is enclosed in and protected by the vertebral column (it passes through the spinal canal). It consists of nerve cells. The spinal cord carries sensory signals and motor innervation to most of the skeletal muscles in the body.
Motor neuron	A motor neuron is an efferent neuron that originates in the spinal cord and synapses with muscle fibers to facilitate muscle contraction and with muscle spindles to modify proprioceptive sensitivity.
Neuron	The neuron is the primary cell of the nervous system. They are found in the brain, the spinal cord, in the nerves and ganglia of the peripheral nervous system. It is a specialized cell that conducts impulses through the nervous system and contains three major parts: cell body, dendrites, and an axon. It can have many dendrites but only one axon.
Skeletal muscle	Skeletal muscle is a type of striated muscle, attached to the skeleton. They are used to facilitate movement, by applying force to bones and joints; via contraction. They generally contract voluntarily (via nerve stimulation), although they can contract involuntarily.
Reticular formation	Reticular formation is a part of the brain which is involved in stereotypical actions, such as walking, sleeping, and lying down. The reticular formation, phylogenetically one of the oldest portions of the brain, is a poorly-differentiated area of the brain stem.

Chapter 6. Wakefulness, Alertness, Sleep, and Dreams

Chapter 6. Wakefulness, Alertness, Sleep, and Dreams

Narcolepsy	A serious sleep disorder characterized by excessive daytime sleepiness and sudden, uncontrollable attacks of REM sleep is called narcolepsy.
Rem rebound	Rem rebound refers to the increased amount of REM sleep that occurs after REM deprivation; often associated with unpleasant dreams or nightmares.
Self-reflection	In Bandura's social cognitive theory, the ability to analyze one's thoughts and actions is referred to as self-reflection.
Threshold	In general, a threshold is a fixed location or value where an abrupt change is observed. In the sensory modalities, it is the minimum amount of stimulus energy necessary to elicit a sensory response.
Infancy	The developmental period that extends from birth to 18 or 24 months is called infancy.
Maturation	The orderly unfolding of traits, as regulated by the genetic code is called maturation.
Disinhibition	A temporary increase in the strength of an extinguished response caused by an unrelated stimulus event is referred to as disinhibition.
Adaptive behavior	An adaptive behavior increases the probability of the individual or organism to survive or exist within its environment.
Endogenous depression	Endogenous depression causes appear to be produced from within, rather than as a reaction to life events.
Antidepressants	Antidepressants are medications used primarily in the treatment of clinical depression. Antidepressants create little if any immediate change in mood and require between several days and several weeks to take effect.
Monoamine oxidase inhibitors	Monoamine oxidase inhibitors are a group of antidepressant drugs that prevent the enzyme monoamine oxidase from deactivating neurotransmitters of the central nervous system.
Monoamine oxidase	Monoamine oxidase is an enzyme that catalyzes the oxidation of monoamines. They are found bound to the outer membrane of mitochondria in most cell types in the body. Because of the vital role that it play in the inactivation of neurotransmitters, dysfunction (too much/too little MAO activity) is thought to be responsible for a number of neurological disorders.
Tricyclic	Tricyclic antidepressants are a class of antidepressant drugs first used in the 1950s. They are named after the drugs' molecular structure, which contains three rings of atoms.
Short-term memory	Short-term memory is that part of memory which stores a limited amount of information for a limited amount of time (roughly 30-45 seconds). The second key concept associated with a short-term memory is that it has a finite capacity.
Long-term memory	Long-term memory is memory that lasts from over 30 seconds to years.
Learning	Learning is a relatively permanent change in behavior that results from experience. Thus, to attribute a behavioral change to learning, the change must be relatively permanent and must result from experience.
Avoidance learning	Avoidance learning describes how a learner develops a pattern that will allow him/her to avoid an aversive location or situation. Avoidance learning takes place when a map is created which allows the learner not to go to the place where the aversive is.
Retention interval	Retention interval is the time between training and testing in which forgetting may occur.
Hypothesis	A specific statement about behavior or mental processes that is testable through research is a hypothesis.

Chapter 6. Wakefulness, Alertness, Sleep, and Dreams

Chapter 6. Wakefulness, Alertness, Sleep, and Dreams

Declarative memory	Declarative memory is the aspect of memory that stores facts and events. It applies to standard textbook learning and knowledge. It is based on pairing the stimulus and the correct response.
Procedural memory	Procedural memory is the long-term memory of skills and procedures, or "how to" knowledge.
Neocortex	The neocortex is part of the cerebral cortex which covers most of the surface of the cerebral hemispheres including the frontal, parietal, occipital, and temporal lobes. Often seen as the hallmark of human intelligence, the role of this structure in the brain appears to be involved in conscious thought, spatial reasoning, and sensory perception.
Stimulus	A change in an environmental condition that elicits a response is a stimulus.
Anxiety	Anxiety is a complex combination of the feeling of fear, apprehension and worry often accompanied by physical sensations such as palpitations, chest pain and/or shortness of breath.
Divergent thinking	A thought process that attempts to generate multiple solutions to problems is called divergent thinking.
Individual differences	Individual differences psychology studies the ways in which individual people differ in their behavior. This is distinguished from other aspects of psychology in that although psychology is ostensibly a study of individuals, modern psychologists invariably study groups.
Schizophrenia	Schizophrenia is characterized by persistent defects in the perception or expression of reality. A person suffering from untreated schizophrenia typically demonstrates grossly disorganized thinking, and may also experience delusions or auditory hallucinations
Reasoning	Reasoning is the act of using reason to derive a conclusion from certain premises. There are two main methods to reach a conclusion, deductive reasoning and inductive reasoning.
Self-concept	Self-concept refers to domain-specific evaluations of the self where a domain may be academics, athletics, etc.
Ego	In Freud's view the Ego serves to balance our primitive needs and our moral beliefs and taboos. Relying on experience, a healthy Ego provides the ability to adapt to reality and interact with the outside world.
Cognitive dissonance	Cognitive dissonance is a state of opposition between cognitions. Contradicting cognitions serve as a driving force that compel the mind to acquire or invent new thoughts or beliefs, or to modify existing beliefs, so as to minimize the amount of dissonance between cognitions.
Control subjects	Control subjects are participants in an experiment who do not receive the treatment effect but for whom all other conditions are held comparable to those of experimental subjects.
Neuroticism	Eysenck's use of the term neuroticism (or Emotional Stability) was proposed as the dimension describing individual differences in the predisposition towards neurotic disorder.
Activation-synthesis	Activation-Synthesis is a neurobiological theory of dreams, put forward by Allan Hobson and Robert McCarley in 1977, which states that dreams are a random event caused by firing of neurons in the brain.
Forebrain	The forebrain is the highest level of the brain. Key structures in the forebrain are the limbic system, thalamus, basal ganglia, hypothalamus, and cerebral cortex.
Hallucination	A hallucination is a sensory perception experienced in the absence of an external stimulus, as distinct from an illusion, which is a misperception of an external stimulus. They may occur in any sensory modality - visual, auditory, olfactory, gustatory, tactile, or mixed.
Delusion	A false belief, not generally shared by others, and that cannot be changed despite strong

Chapter 6. Wakefulness, Alertness, Sleep, and Dreams

Chapter 6. Wakefulness, Alertness, Sleep, and Dreams

	evidence to the contrary is a delusion.
Brain stem	The brain stem is the stalk of the brain below the cerebral hemispheres. It is the major route for communication between the forebrain and the spinal cord and peripheral nerves. It also controls various functions including respiration, regulation of heart rhythms, and primary aspects of sound localization.
Physiological changes	Alterations in heart rate, blood pressure, perspiration, and other involuntary responses are physiological changes.
Limbic system	The limbic system is a group of brain structures that are involved in various emotions such as aggression, fear, pleasure and also in the formation of memory. The limbic system affects the endocrine system and the autonomic nervous system. It consists of several subcortical structures located around the thalamus.
Theories	Theories are logically self-consistent models or frameworks describing the behavior of a certain natural or social phenomenon. They are broad explanations and predictions concerning phenomena of interest.
Guilt	Guilt describes many concepts related to a negative emotion or condition caused by actions which are believed to be, morally wrong. According to Freud, the avoidance of guilt is the basis for moral behavior.
Motives	Needs or desires that energize and direct behavior toward a goal are motives.
Superego	Frued's third psychic structure, which functions as a moral guardian and sets forth high standards for behavior is the superego.
Manifest content	In psychodynamic theory, the reported content of dreams is referred to as manifest content.
Latent content	In psychodynamic theory, the symbolized or underlying content of dreams is called latent content.
Obsession	An obsession is a thought or idea that the sufferer cannot stop thinking about. Common examples include fears of acquiring disease, getting hurt, or causing harm to someone. They are typically automatic, frequent, distressing, and difficult to control or put an end to by themselves.
Nightmare	Nightmare was the original term for the state later known as waking dream, and more currently as sleep paralysis, associated with rapid eye movement (REM) periods of sleep.
Stress disorder	A significant emotional disturbance caused by stresses outside the range of normal human experience is referred to as stress disorder.
Population	Population refers to all members of a well-defined group of organisms, events, or things.
Accommodation	Piaget's developmental process of accommodation is the modification of currently held schemes or new schemes so that new information inconsistent with the existing schemes can be integrated and understood.
Catecholamines	Catecholamines are chemical compounds derived from the amino acid tyrosine that act as hormones or neurotransmitters. High catecholamine levels in blood are associated with stress.
Acquisition	Acquisition is the process of adapting to the environment, learning or becoming conditioned. In classical conditoning terms, it is the initial learning of the stimulus response link, which involves a neutral stimulus being associated with a unconditioned stimulus and becoming a conditioned stimulus.
Insomnia	Insomnia is a sleep disorder characterized by an inability to sleep and/or to remain asleep for a reasonable period during the night.
Socioeconomic	A family's socioeconomic status is based on family income, parental education level, parental

Chapter 6. Wakefulness, Alertness, Sleep, and Dreams

Chapter 6. Wakefulness, Alertness, Sleep, and Dreams

Status	occupation, and social status in the community. Those with high status often have more success in preparing their children for school because they have access to a wide range of resources.
Socioeconomic	Socioeconomic pertains to the study of the social and economic impacts of any product or service offering, market intervention or other activity on an economy as a whole and on the companies, organization and individuals who are its main economic actors.
Barbiturate	A barbiturate is a drug that acts as a central nervous system (CNS) depressant, and by virtue of this produces a wide spectrum of effects, from mild sedation to anesthesia.
Delirium tremens	Delirium tremens refers to a condition characterized by sweating, restlessness, disorientation, and hallucinations. It occurs in some chronic alcohol users when there is a sudden decrease in usage.
Delirium	Delirium is a medical term used to describe an acute decline in attention and cognition. Delirium is probably the single most common acute disorder affecting adults in general hospitals. It affects 10-20% of all adults in hospital, and 30-40% of older patients.
Amphetamine	Amphetamine is a synthetic stimulant used to suppress the appetite, control weight, and treat disorders including narcolepsy and ADHD. It is also used recreationally and for performance enhancement.
Tranquilizer	A sedative, or tranquilizer, is a drug that depresses the central nervous system (CNS), which causes calmness, relaxation, reduction of anxiety, sleepiness, slowed breathing, slurred speech, staggering gait, poor judgment, and slow, uncertain reflexes.
Hypersomnia	Hypersomnia is an excessive amount of sleepiness, resulting in an inability to stay awake. A person is considered to have hypersomnia if he or she sleeps more than 10 hours per day on a regular basis for at least two weeks.
Night terror	A night terror is a parasomnia sleep disorder characterized by extreme terror and a temporary inability to regain full consciousness. The subject wakes abruptly from the fourth stage of sleep, with waking usually accompanied by gasping, moaning, or screaming. It is often impossible to fully awaken the person, and after the episode the subject normally settles back to sleep without waking.
Enuresis	Enuresis is involuntary urination while asleep. It is the normal state of affairs in infancy, but can be a source of embarrassment when it persists into school age or the teen years.
Pathology	Pathology is the study of the processes underlying disease and other forms of illness, harmful abnormality, or dysfunction.
Hypoxia	Hypoxia is a pathological condition in which the body as a whole or region of the body is deprived of adequate oxygen supply.

Chapter 7. Drug Use and Drug Addiction

Hypothesis	A specific statement about behavior or mental processes that is testable through research is a hypothesis.
Self-awareness	Realization that one's existence and functioning are separate from those of other people and things is called self-awareness.
Depression	In everyday language depression refers to any downturn in mood, which may be relatively transitory and perhaps due to something trivial. This is differentiated from Clinical depression which is marked by symptoms that last two weeks or more and are so severe that they interfere with daily living.
Addiction	Addiction is an uncontrollable compulsion to repeat a behavior regardless of its consequences. Many drugs or behaviors can precipitate a pattern of conditions recognized as addiction, which include a craving for more of the drug or behavior, increased physiological tolerance to exposure, and withdrawal symptoms in the absence of the stimulus.
Stimulant	A stimulant is a drug which increases the activity of the sympathetic nervous system and produces a sense of euphoria or awakeness.
Heroin	Heroin is widely and illegally used as a powerful and addictive drug producing intense euphoria, which often disappears with increasing tolerance. Heroin is a semi-synthetic opioid. It is the 3,6-diacetyl derivative of morphine and is synthesised from it by acetylation.
Marijuana	Marijuana is the dried vegetable matter of the Cannabis sativa plant. It contains large concentrations of compounds that have medicinal and psychoactive effects when consumed, usually by smoking or eating.
Nicotine	Nicotine is an organic compound, an alkaloid found naturally throughout the tobacco plant, with a high concentration in the leaves. It is a potent nerve poison and is included in many insecticides. In lower concentrations, the substance is a stimulant and is one of the main factors leading to the pleasure and habit-forming qualities of tobacco smoking.
Adaptation	Adaptation is a lowering of sensitivity to a stimulus following prolonged exposure to that stimulus. Behavioral adaptations are special ways a particular organism behaves to survive in its natural habitat.
Dopamine	Dopamine is critical to the way the brain controls our movements and is a crucial part of the basal ganglia motor loop. It is commonly associated with the 'pleasure system' of the brain, providing feelings of enjoyment and reinforcement to motivate us to do, or continue doing, certain activities.
Learning	Learning is a relatively permanent change in behavior that results from experience. Thus, to attribute a behavioral change to learning, the change must be relatively permanent and must result from experience.
Attention	Attention is the cognitive process of selectively concentrating on one thing while ignoring other things. Psychologists have labeled three types of attention: sustained attention, selective attention, and divided attention.
Adaptive behavior	An adaptive behavior increases the probability of the individual or organism to survive or exist within its environment.
Habit	A habit is a response that has become completely separated from its eliciting stimulus. Early learning theorists used the term to describe S-R associations, however not all S-R associations become a habit, rather many are extinguished after reinforcement is withdrawn.
Chronic	Chronic refers to a relatively long duration, usually more than a few months.
Stages	Stages represent relatively discrete periods of time in which functioning is qualitatively

Chapter 7. Drug Use and Drug Addiction

	different from functioning at other periods.
Motivation	In psychology, motivation is the driving force (desire) behind all actions of an organism.
Personality	Personality refers to the pattern of enduring characteristics that differentiates a person, the patterns of behaviors that make each individual unique.
Substance abuse	Substance abuse refers to the overindulgence in and dependence on a stimulant, depressant, or other chemical substance, leading to effects that are detrimental to the individual's physical or mental health, or the welfare of others.
Affect	A subjective feeling or emotional tone often accompanied by bodily expressions noticeable to others is called affect.
Psychoactive drug	A psychoactive drug or psychotropic substance is a chemical that alters brain function, resulting in temporary changes in perception, mood, consciousness, or behavior. Such drugs are often used for recreational and spiritual purposes, as well as in medicine, especially for treating neurological and psychological illnesses.
Consciousness	The awareness of the sensations, thoughts, and feelings being experienced at a given moment is called consciousness.
Anxiety	Anxiety is a complex combination of the feeling of fear, apprehension and worry often accompanied by physical sensations such as palpitations, chest pain and/or shortness of breath.
Physiological changes	Alterations in heart rate, blood pressure, perspiration, and other involuntary responses are physiological changes.
Baseline	Measure of a particular behavior or process taken before the introduction of the independent variable or treatment is called the baseline.
Disuse	Disuse refers to theory that memory traces weaken when memories are not periodically used or retrieved.
Opiates	A group of narcotics derived from the opium poppy that provide a euphoric rush and depress the nervous system are referred to as opiates.
Barbiturate	A barbiturate is a drug that acts as a central nervous system (CNS) depressant, and by virtue of this produces a wide spectrum of effects, from mild sedation to anesthesia.
Amphetamine	Amphetamine is a synthetic stimulant used to suppress the appetite, control weight, and treat disorders including narcolepsy and ADHD. It is also used recreationally and for performance enhancement.
Cocaine	Cocaine is a crystalline tropane alkaloid that is obtained from the leaves of the coca plant. It is a stimulant of the central nervous system and an appetite suppressant, creating what has been described as a euphoric sense of happiness and increased energy.
Paranoia	In popular culture, the term paranoia is usually used to describe excessive concern about one's own well-being, sometimes suggesting a person holds persecutory beliefs concerning a threat to themselves or their property and is often linked to a belief in conspiracy theories.
Self-esteem	Self-esteem refers to a person's subjective appraisal of himself or herself as intrinsically positive or negative to some degree.
Emotion	An emotion is a mental states that arise spontaneously, rather than through conscious effort. They are often accompanied by physiological changes.
Withdrawal symptoms	Withdrawal symptoms are physiological changes that occur when the use of a drug is stopped or dosage decreased.

Go to **Cram101.com** for the Practice Tests for this Chapter.

Chapter 7. Drug Use and Drug Addiction

Chapter 7. Drug Use and Drug Addiction

Alcoholic	An alcoholic is dependent on alcohol as characterized by craving, loss of control, physical dependence and withdrawal symptoms, and tolerance.
Brain	The brain controls and coordinates most movement, behavior and homeostatic body functions such as heartbeat, blood pressure, fluid balance and body temperature. Functions of the brain are responsible for cognition, emotion, memory, motor learning and other sorts of learning. The brain is primarily made up of two types of cells: glia and neurons.
Consummatory behaviors	Innate survival behaviors such as copulating and eating are referred to as consummatory behaviors.
Extinction	In operant extinction, if no reinforcement is delivered after the response, gradually the behavior will no longer occur in the presence of the stimulus. The process is more rapid following continuous reinforcement rather than after partial reinforcement. In Classical Conditioning, repeated presentations of the CS without being followed by the US results in the extinction of the CS.
Perception	Perception is the process of acquiring, interpreting, selecting, and organizing sensory information.
Antianxiety drugs	Drugs that can reduce a person's level of excitability while increasing feelings of well-being are called antianxiety drugs.
Sensation seeking	A generalized preference for high or low levels of sensory stimulation is referred to as sensation seeking.
Sensation	Sensation is the first stage in the chain of biochemical and neurologic events that begins with the impinging of a stimulus upon the receptor cells of a sensory organ, which then leads to perception, the mental state that is reflected in statements like "I see a uniformly blue wall."
Positive relationship	Statistically, a positive relationship refers to a mathematical relationship in which increases in one measure are matched by increases in the other.
Temperament	Temperament refers to a basic, innate disposition to change behavior. The activity level is an important dimension of temperament.
Arousal theory	Hebb proposed that attention was a function of arousal, the first arousal theory. Hebb proposed that all human beings have a need to maintain their arousal levels and that there is an optimal level for performance.
Feedback	Feedback refers to information returned to a person about the effects a response has had.
Central nervous system	The vertebrate central nervous system consists of the brain and spinal cord.
Nervous system	The body's electrochemical communication circuitry, made up of billions of neurons is a nervous system.
Trait	An enduring personality characteristic that tends to lead to certain behaviors is called a trait. The term trait also means a genetically inherited feature of an organism.
Enzyme	An enzyme is a protein that catalyzes, or speeds up, a chemical reaction. Enzymes are essential to sustain life because most chemical reactions in biological cells would occur too slowly, or would lead to different products, without enzymes.
Monoamine oxidase	Monoamine oxidase is an enzyme that catalyzes the oxidation of monoamines. They are found bound to the outer membrane of mitochondria in most cell types in the body. Because of the vital role that it play in the inactivation of neurotransmitters, dysfunction (too much/too little MAO activity) is thought to be responsible for a number of neurological disorders.

Chapter 7. Drug Use and Drug Addiction

Chapter 7. Drug Use and Drug Addiction

Individual differences	Individual differences psychology studies the ways in which individual people differ in their behavior. This is distinguished from other aspects of psychology in that although psychology is ostensibly a study of individuals, modern psychologists invariably study groups.
Social reinforcement	Praise, attention, approval, and/or affection from others is referred to as social reinforcement.
Reinforcement	In operant conditioning, reinforcement is any change in an environment that (a) occurs after the behavior, (b) seems to make that behavior re-occur more often in the future and (c) that reoccurence of behavior must be the result of the change.
Construct	A generalized concept, such as anxiety or gravity, is a construct.
Limbic system	The limbic system is a group of brain structures that are involved in various emotions such as aggression, fear, pleasure and also in the formation of memory. The limbic system affects the endocrine system and the autonomic nervous system. It consists of several subcortical structures located around the thalamus.
Evolutionary perspective	A perspective that focuses on how humans have evolved and adapted behaviors required for survival against various environmental pressures over the long course is called the evolutionary perspective.
Ventral tegmental area	The ventral tegmental area is part of the midbrain, lying close to the substantia nigra and the red nucleus. It is rich in dopamine and serotonin neurons. It is considered to be part of the pleasure or reward system, one of the major sources of incentive and behavioral motivation.
Nucleus accumbens	A complex of neurons that is part of the brain's "pleasure pathway" responsible for the experience of reward is referred to as the nucleus accumbens.
Nucleus	In neuroanatomy, a cluster of cell bodies of neurons within the central nervous system is a nucleus.
Neurotransmitter	A neurotransmitter is a chemical that is used to relay, amplify and modulate electrical signals between a neurons and another cell.
Reuptake	Reuptake is the reabsorption of a neurotransmitter by the molecular transporter of a pre-synaptic neuron after it has performed its function of transmitting a neural impulse.
Synapse	A synapse is specialized junction through which cells of the nervous system signal to one another and to non-neuronal cells such as muscles or glands.
Morphine	Morphine, the principal active agent in opium, is a powerful opioid analgesic drug. According to recent research, it may also be produced naturally by the human brain. Morphine is usually highly addictive, and tolerance and physical and psychological dependence develop quickly.
Main effects	Any changes in the dependent variable that have resulted from a change in the independent variable are called main effects.
Receptor	A sensory receptor is a structure that recognizes a stimulus in the internal or external environment of an organism. In response to stimuli the sensory receptor initiates sensory transduction by creating graded potentials or action potentials in the same cell or in an adjacent one.
Pituitary gland	The pituitary gland is an endocrine gland about the size of a pea that sits in the small, bony cavity at the base of the brain. The pituitary gland secretes hormones regulating a wide variety of bodily activities, including trophic hormones that stimulate other endocrine glands.
Gland	A gland is an organ in an animal's body that synthesizes a substance for release such as hormones, often into the bloodstream or into cavities inside the body or its outer surface.

Chapter 7. Drug Use and Drug Addiction

Chapter 7. Drug Use and Drug Addiction

Hormone	A hormone is a chemical messenger from one cell (or group of cells) to another. The best known are those produced by endocrine glands, but they are produced by nearly every organ system. The function of hormones is to serve as a signal to the target cells; the action of the hormone is determined by the pattern of secretion and the signal transduction of the receiving tissue.
Endorphin	An endorphin is an endogenous opioid biochemical compound. They are peptides produced by the pituitary gland and the hypothalamus, and they resemble the opiates in their abilities to produce analgesia and a sense of well-being. In other words, they work as "natural pain killers."
Opioid	An opioid is any agent that binds to opioid receptors, found principally in the central nervous system and gastrointestinal tract.
Receptor site	A location on the dendrite of a receiving neuron that is tailored to receive a specific neurotransmitter is a receptor site.
Methadone	Methadone is a synthetic heroin substitute used for treating heroin addicts that acts as a substitute for heroin by eliminating its effects and the craving for it. Just like heroin, tolerance and dependence frequently develop.
Placebo	Placebo refers to a bogus treatment that has the appearance of being genuine.
Conditioning	Conditioning describes the process by which behaviors can be learned or modified through interaction with the environment.
Population	Population refers to all members of a well-defined group of organisms, events, or things.
Illusion	An illusion is a distortion of a sensory perception.
Variable	A variable refers to a measurable factor, characteristic, or attribute of an individual or a system.
Cannabis	The hemp plant from which marijuana, hashish, and THC are derived is the cannabis.
Species	Species refers to a reproductively isolated breeding population.
Reaction time	The amount of time required to respond to a stimulus is referred to as reaction time.
Blocking	If the one of the two members of a compound stimulus fails to produce the CR due to an earlier conditioning of the other member of the compound stimulus, blocking has occurred.
Norepinephrine	Norepinephrine is released from the adrenal glands as a hormone into the blood, but it is also a neurotransmitter in the nervous system. As a stress hormone, it affects parts of the human brain where attention and impulsivity are controlled. Along with epinephrine, this compound effects the fight-or-flight response, activating the sympathetic nervous system to directly increase heart rate, release energy from fat, and increase muscle readiness.
Metabolism	Metabolism is the biochemical modification of chemical compounds in living organisms and cells.
Incentive	An incentive is what is expected once a behavior is performed. An incentive acts as a reinforcer.
Creativity	Creativity is the ability to think about something in novel and unusual ways and come up with unique solutions to problems. It involves divergent thinking, having many solutions or views to a problem.
Hallucination	A hallucination is a sensory perception experienced in the absence of an external stimulus, as distinct from an illusion, which is a misperception of an external stimulus. They may occur in any sensory modality - visual, auditory, olfactory, gustatory, tactile, or mixed.

Go to **Cram101.com** for the Practice Tests for this Chapter.

Chapter 7. Drug Use and Drug Addiction

Body image	A person's body image is their perception of their physical appearance. It is more than what a person thinks they will see in a mirror, it is inextricably tied to their self-esteem and acceptance by peers.
Depersonaliztion	Depersonalization is the experience of feelings of loss of a sense of reality. A sufferer feels that they have changed and the world has become less real — it is vague, dreamlike, or lacking in significance.
Anandamide	Anandamide is a naturally occurring neurotransmitter found in the brain of animals, as well as other organs. Anandamide receptors were originally discovered as being sensitive to tetrahydrocannabinol, which is among the psychoactive cannabinoids found in marijuana.
Reticular activating system	The reticular activating system is the part of the brain believed to be the center of arousal and motivation. It is situated between the brain stem and the central nervous system (CNS).
Neuron	The neuron is the primary cell of the nervous system. They are found in the brain, the spinal cord, in the nerves and ganglia of the peripheral nervous system. It is a specialized cell that conducts impulses through the nervous system and contains three major parts: cell body, dendrites, and an axon. It can have many dendrites but only one axon.
Serotonin	Serotonin, a neurotransmitter, is believed to play an important part of the biochemistry of depression, bipolar disorder and anxiety. It is also believed to be influential on sexuality and appetite.
Psilocybin	A psychedelic drug extracted from the mushroom Psilocybe mexicana is called psilocybin. At low doses, hallucinatory effects occur, including walls that seem to breathe, a vivid enhancement of colors and the animation of organic shapes. At higher doses, experiences tend to be less social and more entheogenic, often catalyzing intense spiritual experiences.
Forethought	Forethought is a person's capability to motivate themselves and guide their actions anticipatorily. Stimuli are not automatically linked to the response by contiguity. Instead, previous experiences create expectations of the outcome that will occur as a result of performing a behavior, before the behavior is performed.
Psychedelic	A psychedelic experience is characterized by the perception of aspects of one's mind previously unknown, or by the creative exuberance of the mind.
Tactile	Pertaining to the sense of touch is referred to as tactile.
MDMA	MDMA, most commonly known today by the street name ecstasy, is a synthetic entactogen of the phenethylamine family whose primary effect is to stimulate the secretion of large amounts of serotonin as well as dopamine and noradrenaline in the brain, causing a general sense of openness, empathy, energy, euphoria, and well-being.
Hallucinogenic	Certain drugs can affect the subjective qualities of perception, thought or emotion, resulting in altered interpretations of sensory input, alternate states of consciousness, or hallucinations. The term hallucinogenic is often broadly applied, especially in current scientific literature, to some or all of these substances.
Epilepsy	Epilepsy is a chronic neurological condition characterized by recurrent unprovoked neural discharges. It is commonly controlled with medication, although surgical methods are used as well.
Multiple sclerosis	Multiple sclerosis affects neurons, the cells of the brain and spinal cord that carry information, create thought and perception, and allow the brain to control the body. Surrounding and protecting these neurons is a layer of fat, called myelin, which helps neurons carry electrical signals. MS causes gradual destruction of myelin (demyelination) in patches throughout the brain and/or spinal cord, causing various symptoms depending upon

Chapter 7. Drug Use and Drug Addiction

Chapter 7. Drug Use and Drug Addiction

	which signals are interrupted.
Mood disorder	A mood disorder is a condition where the prevailing emotional mood is distorted or inappropriate to the circumstances.
Disinhibition	A temporary increase in the strength of an extinguished response caused by an unrelated stimulus event is referred to as disinhibition.
Cognition	The intellectual processes through which information is obtained, transformed, stored, retrieved, and otherwise used is cognition.
Glucose	Glucose, a simple monosaccharide sugar, is one of the most important carbohydrates and is used as a source of energy in animals and plants. Glucose is one of the main products of photosynthesis and starts respiration.
Cerebellum	The cerebellum is located in the inferior posterior portion of the head (the hindbrain), directly dorsal to the brainstem and pons, inferior to the occipital lobe. The cerebellum is a region of the brain that plays an important role in the integration of sensory perception and fine motor output.
Suppression	Suppression is the defense mechanism where a memory is deliberately forgotten.
Depressant	A depressant is a chemical agent that diminishes a body function or activity. The term is used in particular with regard to the central nervous system where these chemicals are known as neurotransmitters. They tend to act on the CNS by increasing the activity of a particular neurotransmitter known as gamma-aminobutyric acid (GABA).
Stimulus	A change in an environmental condition that elicits a response is a stimulus.
Experimental neurosis	Any bizarre or neurotic-like behavior induced through an experimental procedure such as discrimination training is called experimental neurosis.
Neurosis	Neurosis, any mental disorder that, although may cause distress, does not interfere with rational thought or the persons' ability to function.
Approach/avoidance conflict	Approach/avoidance conflict refers to the tension experienced by people when they are simultaneously attracted to and repulsed by the same goal.
Goal-directed behavior	Goal-directed behavior is means-end problem solving behavior. In the infant, such behavior is first observed in the latter part of the first year.
Testosterone	Testosterone is a steroid hormone from the androgen group. It is the principal male sex hormone and the "original" anabolic steroid.
Alcoholism	A disorder that involves long-term, repeated, uncontrolled, compulsive, and excessive use of alcoholic beverages and that impairs the drinker's health and work and social relationships is called alcoholism.
Conduct disorder	Conduct disorder is the psychiatric diagnostic category for the occurrence of multiple delinquent activities over a 6-month period. These behaviors include truancy, running away, fire setting, cruelty to animals, breaking and entering, and excessive fighting.
Antisocial personality disorder	A disorder in which individuals tend to display no regard for the moral and ethical rules of society or the rights of others is called antisocial personality disorder.
Personality disorder	A mental disorder characterized by a set of inflexible, maladaptive personality traits that keep a person from functioning properly in society is referred to as a personality disorder.
Genetics	Genetics is the science of genes, heredity, and the variation of organisms.
Myopia	Myopia is a refractive defect of the eye in which light focuses in front of the retina. Those

Chapter 7. Drug Use and Drug Addiction

Chapter 7. Drug Use and Drug Addiction

	with myopia are often described as nearsighted or short-sighted in that they typically can see nearby objects clearly but distant objects appear blurred because the lens cannot flatten enough.
Information processing	Information processing is an approach to the goal of understanding human thinking. The essence of the approach is to see cognition as being essentially computational in nature, with mind being the software and the brain being the hardware.
Ego	In Freud's view the Ego serves to balance our primitive needs and our moral beliefs and taboos. Relying on experience, a healthy Ego provides the ability to adapt to reality and interact with the outside world.
Self-image	A person's self-image is the mental picture, generally of a kind that is quite resistant to change, that depicts not only details that are potentially available to objective investigation by others, but also items that have been learned by that person about himself or herself.
Theories	Theories are logically self-consistent models or frameworks describing the behavior of a certain natural or social phenomenon. They are broad explanations and predictions concerning phenomena of interest.
Control group	A group that does not receive the treatment effect in an experiment is referred to as the control group or sometimes as the comparison group.
Controlled drinking	A behavioral approach to the treatment of alcoholism, designed to teach the skills necessary so that alcoholics can drink socially without losing control is referred to as controlled drinking.
Modeling	A type of behavior learned through observation of others demonstrating the same behavior is modeling.
Ethnicity	Ethnicity refers to a characteristic based on cultural heritage, nationality characteristics, race, religion, and language.
Self-efficacy	Self-efficacy is the belief that one has the capabilities to execute the courses of actions required to manage prospective situations.
Attitude	An enduring mental representation of a person, place, or thing that evokes an emotional response and related behavior is called attitude.
Achievement motivation	The psychological need in humans for success is called achievement motivation.

Chapter 7. Drug Use and Drug Addiction

Chapter 8. Aggression, Coercive Action, and Anger

Adaptation	Adaptation is a lowering of sensitivity to a stimulus following prolonged exposure to that stimulus. Behavioral adaptations are special ways a particular organism behaves to survive in its natural habitat.
Brain	The brain controls and coordinates most movement, behavior and homeostatic body functions such as heartbeat, blood pressure, fluid balance and body temperature. Functions of the brain are responsible for cognition, emotion, memory, motor learning and other sorts of learning. The brain is primarily made up of two types of cells: glia and neurons.
Deprivation	Deprivation, is the loss or withholding of normal stimulation, nutrition, comfort, love, and so forth; a condition of lacking. The level of stimulation is less than what is required.
Gene	A gene is an ultramicroscopic area of the chromosome. It is the smallest physical unit of the DNA molecule that carries a piece of hereditary information.
Empirical	Empirical means the use of working hypotheses which are capable of being disproved using observation or experiment.
Motivation	In psychology, motivation is the driving force (desire) behind all actions of an organism.
Attitude	An enduring mental representation of a person, place, or thing that evokes an emotional response and related behavior is called attitude.
Social skills	Social skills are skills used to interact and communicate with others to assist status in the social structure and other motivations.
Theories	Theories are logically self-consistent models or frameworks describing the behavior of a certain natural or social phenomenon. They are broad explanations and predictions concerning phenomena of interest.
Learning	Learning is a relatively permanent change in behavior that results from experience. Thus, to attribute a behavioral change to learning, the change must be relatively permanent and must result from experience.
Emotion	An emotion is a mental states that arise spontaneously, rather than through conscious effort. They are often accompanied by physiological changes.
Threshold	In general, a threshold is a fixed location or value where an abrupt change is observed. In the sensory modalities, it is the minimum amount of stimulus energy necessary to elicit a sensory response.
Positive correlation	A relationship between two variables in which both vary in the same direction is called a positive correlation.
Correlation	A statistical technique for determining the degree of association between two or more variables is referred to as correlation.
Self-report inventories	Personality tests that ask individuals to answer a series of questions about their own characteristic behaviors are called self-report inventories.
Factor analysis	Factor analysis is a statistical technique that originated in psychometrics. The objective is to explain the most of the variability among a number of observable random variables in terms of a smaller number of unobservable random variables called factors.
Dizygotic	Fraternal twins (commonly known as "non-identical twins") usually occur when two fertilized eggs are implanted in the uterine wall at the same time. The two eggs form two zygotes, and these twins are therefore also known as dizygotic.
Monozygotic	Identical twins occur when a single egg is fertilized to form one zygote, calld monozygotic, but the zygote then divides into two separate embryos. The two embryos develop into foetuses sharing the same womb. Monozygotic twins are genetically identical unless there has been a

Chapter 8. Aggression, Coercive Action, and Anger

Chapter 8. Aggression, Coercive Action, and Anger

	mutation in development, and they are almost always the same gender.
Meta-analysis	In statistics, a meta-analysis combines the results of several studies that address a set of related research hypotheses.
Personality	Personality refers to the pattern of enduring characteristics that differentiates a person, the patterns of behaviors that make each individual unique.
Genetics	Genetics is the science of genes, heredity, and the variation of organisms.
Variance	The degree to which scores differ among individuals in a distribution of scores is the variance.
Trait	An enduring personality characteristic that tends to lead to certain behaviors is called a trait. The term trait also means a genetically inherited feature of an organism.
Serotonin	Serotonin, a neurotransmitter, is believed to play an important part of the biochemistry of depression, bipolar disorder and anxiety. It is also believed to be influential on sexuality and appetite.
Temperament	Temperament refers to a basic, innate disposition to change behavior. The activity level is an important dimension of temperament.
Hormone	A hormone is a chemical messenger from one cell (or group of cells) to another. The best known are those produced by endocrine glands, but they are produced by nearly every organ system. The function of hormones is to serve as a signal to the target cells; the action of the hormone is determined by the pattern of secretion and the signal transduction of the receiving tissue.
Testosterone	Testosterone is a steroid hormone from the androgen group. It is the principal male sex hormone and the "original" anabolic steroid.
Random assignment	Assignment of participants to experimental and control groups by chance is called random assignment. Random assigment reduces the likelihood that the results are due to preexisiting systematic differences between the groups.
Castration	Castration is any action, surgical, chemical or otherwise, by which a biological male loses use of the testes. This causes sterilization, i.e. prevents him from reproducing; it also greatly reduces the production of certain hormones, such as testosterone.
Trauma	Trauma refers to a severe physical injury or wound to the body caused by an external force, or a psychological shock having a lasting effect on mental life.
Estradiol	Estradiol is a sex hormone. Labelled the "female" hormone but also present in males it represents the major estrogen in humans. Critical for sexual functioning estradiol also supports bone growth.
Androgen	Androgen is the generic term for any natural or synthetic compound, usually a steroid hormone, that stimulates or controls the development and maintenance of masculine characteristics in vertebrates by binding to androgen receptors.
Clitoris	Clitoris refers to an external female sex organ that is highly sensitive to sexual stimulation.
Gonads	The gonads are the organs that make gametes. Gametes are haploid germ cells. For example, sperm and egg cells are gametes. In the male the gonads are the testicles, and in the female the gonads are the ovaries.
Adrenal glands	The adrenal glands sit atop the kidneys. They are chiefly responsible for regulating the stress response through the synthesis of corticosteroids and catecholamines, including cortisol and adrenalin.

Chapter 8. Aggression, Coercive Action, and Anger

Chapter 8. Aggression, Coercive Action, and Anger

Gland	A gland is an organ in an animal's body that synthesizes a substance for release such as hormones, often into the bloodstream or into cavities inside the body or its outer surface.
Bisexuality	Bisexuality is a sexual orientation characterized by aesthetic attraction, romantic love and sexual desire for both males and females.
Genitals	Genitals refers to the internal and external reproductive organs.
Statistics	Statistics is a type of data analysis which practice includes the planning, summarizing, and interpreting of observations of a system possibly followed by predicting or forecasting of future events based on a mathematical model of the system being observed.
Statistic	A statistic is an observable random variable of a sample.
Standard deviation	In probability and statistics, the standard deviation is the most commonly used measure of statistical dispersion. Simply put, it measures how spread out the values in a data set are.
Questionnaire	A self-report method of data collection or clinical assessment method in which the individual being studied checks off items on a printed list, answers multiple-choice questions, or writes out answers to essay questions aimed at producing a selfdescription is called questionnaire.
Paradigm	Paradigm refers to the set of practices that defines a scientific discipline during a particular period of time. It provides a framework from which to conduct research, it ensures that a certain range of phenomena, those on which the paradigm focuses, are explored thoroughly. Itmay also blind scientists to other, perhaps more fruitful, ways of dealing with their subject matter.
Guilt	Guilt describes many concepts related to a negative emotion or condition caused by actions which are believed to be, morally wrong. According to Freud, the avoidance of guilt is the basis for moral behavior.
Anxiety	Anxiety is a complex combination of the feeling of fear, apprehension and worry often accompanied by physical sensations such as palpitations, chest pain and/or shortness of breath.
Stereotype	A stereotype is considered to be a group concept, held by one social group about another.They are often used in a negative or prejudicial sense and are frequently used to justify certain discriminatory behaviors. This allows powerful social groups to legitimize and protect their dominant position
Amygdala	Located in the brain's medial temporal lobe, the almond-shaped amygdala is believed to play a key role in the emotions. It forms part of the limbic system and is linked to both fear responses and pleasure. Its size is positively correlated with aggressive behavior across species.
Hypothalamus	The hypothalamus is a region of the brain located below the thalamus, forming the major portion of the ventral region of the diencephalon and functioning to regulate certain metabolic processes and other autonomic activities.
Midbrain	Located between the hindbrain and forebrain, a region in which many nerve-fiber systems ascend and descend to connect the higher and lower portions of the brain is referred to as midbrain. It is archipallian in origin, meaning its general architecture is shared with the most ancient of vertebrates. Dopamine produced in the subtantia nigra plays a role in motivation and habituation of species from humans to the most elementary animals such as insects.
Brain stem	The brain stem is the stalk of the brain below the cerebral hemispheres. It is the major route for communication between the forebrain and the spinal cord and peripheral nerves. It also controls various functions including respiration, regulation of heart rhythms, and

Chapter 8. Aggression, Coercive Action, and Anger

	primary aspects of sound localization.
Punishment	Punishment is the addtion of a stimulus that reduces the frequency of a response, or the removal of a stimulus that results in a reduction of the response.
Instrumental behaviors	Instrumental behaviors refer to behaviors directed toward the achievement of some goal; the behaviors that are instrumental in producing some effect.
Behavioral inhibition system	The behavioral inhibition system is a circuit in the limbic system that responds to threat signals by inhibiting activity and causing anxiety.
Behavioral inhibition	Physiological probes of children with behavioral inhibition show significantly higher measures of activity in the sympathetic nervous system and hypothalamic-pituitary axis than in non-inhibited children. Kagan postulates that anxiety-prone children are born with a lower firing threshold in amygdala and hypothalamic neurons. His work provides a robust model for predicting temperamental forerunners of anxiety disorders.
Attention	Attention is the cognitive process of selectively concentrating on one thing while ignoring other things. Psychologists have labeled three types of attention: sustained attention, selective attention, and divided attention.
Limbic system	The limbic system is a group of brain structures that are involved in various emotions such as aggression, fear, pleasure and also in the formation of memory. The limbic system affects the endocrine system and the autonomic nervous system. It consists of several subcortical structures located around the thalamus.
Hippocampus	The hippocampus is a part of the brain located inside the temporal lobe. It forms a part of the limbic system and plays a part in memory and navigation.
Thalamus	An area near the center of the brain involved in the relay of sensory information to the cortex and in the functions of sleep and attention is the thalamus.
Neuroendocrine system	The network of neurons and glands that make and secrete hormones are referred to as the neuroendocrine system.
Olfactory bulb	The olfactory bulb is a part of the brain that is a distinct outgrowth from the forebrain. It plays a major role in olfaction, which is the perception of smells. The olfactory bulb receives direct input from olfactory nerve, made up of the axons from approximately 10 million olfactory receptor neurons in the olfactory mucosa, a region of the nasal cavity.
Cardiovascular system	The human cardiovascular system comprises the blood, the heart, and a dual-circuit system of blood vessels that serve as conduits between the heart, the lungs, and the peripheral tissues of the body.
Norepinephrine	Norepinephrine is released from the adrenal glands as a hormone into the blood, but it is also a neurotransmitter in the nervous system. As a stress hormone, it affects parts of the human brain where attention and impulsivity are controlled. Along with epinephrine, this compound effects the fight-or-flight response, activating the sympathetic nervous system to directly increase heart rate, release energy from fat, and increase muscle readiness.
Neocortex	The neocortex is part of the cerebral cortex which covers most of the surface of the cerebral hemispheres including the frontal, parietal, occipital, and temporal lobes. Often seen as the hallmark of human intelligence, the role of this structure in the brain appears to be involved in conscious thought, spatial reasoning, and sensory perception.
Stimulus	A change in an environmental condition that elicits a response is a stimulus.
Tumor	A tumor is an abnormal growth that when located in the brain can either be malignant and directly destroy brain tissue, or be benign and disrupt functioning by increasing

Chapter 8. Aggression, Coercive Action, and Anger

Chapter 8. Aggression, Coercive Action, and Anger

	intracranial pressure.
Psychosurgery	Psychosurgery is a term for surgeries of the brain or autonomic nervous system involving the severance of neural pathways to effect a change in behavior, usually to treat or alleviate severe mental illness. The procedures typically considered psychosurgery are now almost universally shunned as inappropriate, due in part to the emergence of less-invasive methods of treatment such as psychiatric medication.
Temporal lobe	The temporal lobe is part of the cerebrum. It lies at the side of the brain, beneath the lateral or Sylvian fissure. Adjacent areas in the superior, posterior and lateral parts of the temporal lobe are involved in high-level auditory processing.
Lobes	The four major sections of the cerebral cortex: frontal, parietal, temporal, and occipital are called lobes.
Estrogen	Estrogen is a group of steroid compounds that function as the primary female sex hormone. They are produced primarily by developing follicles in the ovaries, the corpus luteum and the placenta.
Progesterone	A female sex hormone that promotes growth of the sex organs and helps maintain pregnancy is called progesterone.
Fight-or-flight	The fight-or-flight response, also called the "acute stress response", was first described by Walter Cannon. Animals react to threats with a general discharge of the sympathetic nervous system. In layman's terms, an animal has two options when faced with danger. They can either face the threat, or they can avoid the threat.
Hypothesis	A specific statement about behavior or mental processes that is testable through research is a hypothesis.
Perception	Perception is the process of acquiring, interpreting, selecting, and organizing sensory information.
Motivational state	A motivational state is an internal, reversible condition in an individual that orients the individual toward one or another type of goal. This condition is not observed directly but is inferred from the individual's behavior.
Affect	A subjective feeling or emotional tone often accompanied by bodily expressions noticeable to others is called affect.
Reinforcement	In operant conditioning, reinforcement is any change in an environment that (a) occurs after the behavior, (b) seems to make that behavior re-occur more often in the future and (c) that reoccurence of behavior must be the result of the change.
Partial reinforcement	In a partial reinforcement environment, not every correct response is reinforced. Partial reinforcement is usually introduced after a continuous reinforcement schedule has acquired the behavior.
Generalization	In conditioning, the tendency for a conditioned response to be evoked by stimuli that are similar to the stimulus to which the response was conditioned is a generalization. The greater the similarity among the stimuli, the greater the probability of generalization.
Prototype	A concept of a category of objects or events that serves as a good example of the category is called a prototype.
Primary emotions	Primary emotions, according to Robert Plutchik's theory, are the most basic emotions which include fear, surprise, sadness, disgust, anger, anticipation, joy, and acceptance. Each has high survival value.
Sensation	Sensation is the first stage in the chain of biochemical and neurologic events that begins with the impinging of a stimulus upon the receptor cells of a sensory organ, which then leads

Chapter 8. Aggression, Coercive Action, and Anger

Chapter 8. Aggression, Coercive Action, and Anger

	to perception, the mental state that is reflected in statements like "I see a uniformly blue wall."
Social learning theory	Social learning theory explains the process of gender typing in terms of observation, imitation, and role playing.
Social learning	Social learning is learning that occurs as a function of observing, retaining and replicating behavior observed in others. Although social learning can occur at any stage in life, it is thought to be particularly important during childhood, particularly as authority becomes important.
Acquisition	Acquisition is the process of adapting to the environment, learning or becoming conditioned. In classical conditoning terms, it is the initial learning of the stimulus response link, which involves a neutral stimulus being associated with a unconditioned stimulus and becoming a conditioned stimulus.
Sexual abuse	Sexual abuse is a term used to describe non- consental sexual relations between two or more parties which are considered criminally and/or morally offensive.
Habit	A habit is a response that has become completely separated from its eliciting stimulus. Early learning theorists used the term to describe S-R associations, however not all S-R associations become a habit, rather many are extinguished after reinforcement is withdrawn.
Modeling	A type of behavior learned through observation of others demonstrating the same behavior is modeling.
Rape	Rape is a crime where the victim is forced into sexual activity, in particular sexual penetration, against his or her will.
Goal-directed behavior	Goal-directed behavior is means-end problem solving behavior. In the infant, such behavior is first observed in the latter part of the first year.
Motives	Needs or desires that energize and direct behavior toward a goal are motives.
Negative correlation	A negative correlation refers to a relationship between two variables in which one variable increases as the other decreases.
Information processing	Information processing is an approach to the goal of understanding human thinking. The essence of the approach is to see cognition as being essentially computational in nature, with mind being the software and the brain being the hardware.
Disinhibition	A temporary increase in the strength of an extinguished response caused by an unrelated stimulus event is referred to as disinhibition.
Myopia	Myopia is a refractive defect of the eye in which light focuses in front of the retina. Those with myopia are often described as nearsighted or short-sighted in that they typically can see nearby objects clearly but distant objects appear blurred because the lens cannot flatten enough.
Norms	In testing, standards of test performance that permit the comparison of one person's score on the test to the scores of others who have taken the same test are referred to as norms.
Distributive justice	Distributive justice concerns what is just or right with respect to the allocation of goods (or utility) in a society. Distributive justice concentrates on just outcomes.
Conformity	Conformity is the degree to which members of a group will change their behavior, views and attitudes to fit the views of the group. The group can influence members via unconscious processes or via overt social pressure on individuals.
Lesbian	A lesbian is a homosexual woman. They are women who are sexually and romantically attracted to other women.

Chapter 8. Aggression, Coercive Action, and Anger

Chapter 8. Aggression, Coercive Action, and Anger

Procedural justice	Procedural justice concerns the fairness of the processes by which decisions are made.
Empathy	Empathy is the recognition and understanding of the states of mind, including beliefs, desires and particularly emotions of others without injecting your own.
Adaptive behavior	An adaptive behavior increases the probability of the individual or organism to survive or exist within its environment.
Gender difference	A gender difference is a disparity between genders involving quality or quantity. Though some gender differences are controversial, they are not to be confused with sexist stereotypes.
Adolescence	The period of life bounded by puberty and the assumption of adult responsibilities is adolescence.
Late adolescence	Late adolescence refers to approximately the latter half of the second decade of life. Career interests, dating, and identity exploration are often more pronounced in late adolescence than in early adolescence.
Early adulthood	The developmental period beginning in the late teens or early twenties and lasting into the thirties is called early adulthood; characterized by an increasing self-awareness.
Evolutionary psychology	Evolutionary psychology proposes that cognition and behavior can be better understood in light of evolutionary history.
Maturation	The orderly unfolding of traits, as regulated by the genetic code is called maturation.
Puberty	Puberty refers to the process of physical changes by which a child's body becomes an adult body capable of reproduction.
Socialization	Social rules and social relations are created, communicated, and changed in verbal and nonverbal ways creating social complexity useful in identifying outsiders and intelligent breeding partners. The process of learning these skills is called socialization.
Self-esteem	Self-esteem refers to a person's subjective appraisal of himself or herself as intrinsically positive or negative to some degree.
Nurture	Nurture refers to the environmental influences on behavior due to nutrition, culture, socioeconomic status, and learning.
Self-concept	Self-concept refers to domain-specific evaluations of the self where a domain may be academics, athletics, etc.
Ego	In Freud's view the Ego serves to balance our primitive needs and our moral beliefs and taboos. Relying on experience, a healthy Ego provides the ability to adapt to reality and interact with the outside world.
Juvenile delinquency	Juvenile delinquency refers to a broad range of child and adolescent behaviors, including socially unacceptable behavior, status offenses, and criminal acts.

Chapter 8. Aggression, Coercive Action, and Anger

Chapter 9. Emotions, Stress, and Health

Emotion	An emotion is a mental states that arise spontaneously, rather than through conscious effort. They are often accompanied by physiological changes.
Affect	A subjective feeling or emotional tone often accompanied by bodily expressions noticeable to others is called affect.
Attention	Attention is the cognitive process of selectively concentrating on one thing while ignoring other things. Psychologists have labeled three types of attention: sustained attention, selective attention, and divided attention.
Immune system	The most important function of the human immune system occurs at the cellular level of the blood and tissues. The lymphatic and blood circulation systems are highways for specialized white blood cells. These cells include B cells, T cells, natural killer cells, and macrophages. All function with the primary objective of recognizing, attacking and destroying bacteria, viruses, cancer cells, and all substances seen as foreign.
Motivation	In psychology, motivation is the driving force (desire) behind all actions of an organism.
Perception	Perception is the process of acquiring, interpreting, selecting, and organizing sensory information.
Variable	A variable refers to a measurable factor, characteristic, or attribute of an individual or a system.
Theories	Theories are logically self-consistent models or frameworks describing the behavior of a certain natural or social phenomenon. They are broad explanations and predictions concerning phenomena of interest.
Learning	Learning is a relatively permanent change in behavior that results from experience. Thus, to attribute a behavioral change to learning, the change must be relatively permanent and must result from experience.
Countercondi- tioning	The process of eliminating a classically conditioned response by pairing the CS with an unconditioned stimulus for a response that is stronger than the conditioned response and that cannot occur at the same time as the CR is called counterconditioning.
Goal-directed behavior	Goal-directed behavior is means-end problem solving behavior. In the infant, such behavior is first observed in the latter part of the first year.
Basic emotions	Basic emotions are those found in all cultures, as evidenced by the same facial expressions. They include: fear, anger, disgust, surprise, happiness, and distress.
Law of effect	The law of effect is a principle of psychology described by Edward Thorndike in 1898. It holds that responses to stimuli that produce a satisfying or pleasant effect in a particular situation are more likely to occur again in the situation. Conversely, responses that produce a discomforting or unpleasant effect are less likely to occur again in the situation
Heredity	Heredity is the transfer of characteristics from parent to offspring through their genes.
Motives	Needs or desires that energize and direct behavior toward a goal are motives.
Individual differences	Individual differences psychology studies the ways in which individual people differ in their behavior. This is distinguished from other aspects of psychology in that although psychology is ostensibly a study of individuals, modern psychologists invariably study groups.
Adaptive behavior	An adaptive behavior increases the probability of the individual or organism to survive or exist within its environment.
Eustress	Selye called negative stress distress and positive stress eustress.
Fight-or-flight	The fight-or-flight response, also called the "acute stress response", was first described by Walter Cannon. Animals react to threats with a general discharge of the sympathetic nervous

Chapter 9. Emotions, Stress, and Health

Chapter 9. Emotions, Stress, and Health

	system. In layman's terms, an animal has two options when faced with danger. They can either face the threat, or they can avoid the threat.
Brain	The brain controls and coordinates most movement, behavior and homeostatic body functions such as heartbeat, blood pressure, fluid balance and body temperature. Functions of the brain are responsible for cognition, emotion, memory, motor learning and other sorts of learning. The brain is primarily made up of two types of cells: glia and neurons.
Sympathetic	The sympathetic nervous system activates what is often termed the "fight or flight response". It is an automatic regulation system, that is, one that operates without the intervention of conscious thought.
Adrenal medulla	Composed mainly of hormone-producing chromaffin cells, the adrenal medulla is the principal site of the conversion of the amino acid tyrosine into the catecholamines epinephrine and norepinephrine (also called adrenaline and noradrenaline, respectively).
Gland	A gland is an organ in an animal's body that synthesizes a substance for release such as hormones, often into the bloodstream or into cavities inside the body or its outer surface.
Epinephrine	Epinephrine is a hormone and a neurotransmitter. Epinephrine plays a central role in the short-term stress reaction—the physiological response to threatening or exciting conditions. It is secreted by the adrenal medulla. When released into the bloodstream, epinephrine binds to multiple receptors and has numerous effects throughout the body.
Norepinephrine	Norepinephrine is released from the adrenal glands as a hormone into the blood, but it is also a neurotransmitter in the nervous system. As a stress hormone, it affects parts of the human brain where attention and impulsivity are controlled. Along with epinephrine, this compound effects the fight-or-flight response, activating the sympathetic nervous system to directly increase heart rate, release energy from fat, and increase muscle readiness.
Adrenal cortex	Adrenal cortex refers to the outer layer of the adrenal glands, which produces hormones that affect salt intake, reactions to stress, and sexual development.
Hormone	A hormone is a chemical messenger from one cell (or group of cells) to another. The best known are those produced by endocrine glands, but they are produced by nearly every organ system. The function of hormones is to serve as a signal to the target cells; the action of the hormone is determined by the pattern of secretion and the signal transduction of the receiving tissue.
Cortisol	Cortisol is a corticosteroid hormone that is involved in the response to stress; it increases blood pressure and blood sugar levels and suppresses the immune system. Synthetic cortisol, also known as hydrocortisone, is used as a drug mainly to fight allergies and inflammation.
Endocrine gland	An endocrine gland is one of a set of internal organs involved in the secretion of hormones into the blood. The other major type of gland is the exocrine glands, which secrete substances—usually digestive juices—into the digestive tract or onto the skin.
Hypothalamus	The hypothalamus is a region of the brain located below the thalamus, forming the major portion of the ventral region of the diencephalon and functioning to regulate certain metabolic processes and other autonomic activities.
Central nervous system	The vertebrate central nervous system consists of the brain and spinal cord.
Nervous system	The body's electrochemical communication circuitry, made up of billions of neurons is a nervous system.
Endocrine system	The endocrine system is a control system of ductless endocrine glands that secrete chemical messengers called hormones that circulate within the body via the bloodstream to affect distant organs. It does not include exocrine glands such as salivary glands, sweat glands and

Chapter 9. Emotions, Stress, and Health

	glands within the gastrointestinal tract.
Glucose	Glucose, a simple monosaccharide sugar, is one of the most important carbohydrates and is used as a source of energy in animals and plants. Glucose is one of the main products of photosynthesis and starts respiration.
Pituitary gland	The pituitary gland is an endocrine gland about the size of a pea that sits in the small, bony cavity at the base of the brain. The pituitary gland secretes hormones regulating a wide variety of bodily activities, including trophic hormones that stimulate other endocrine glands.
Analgesia	Analgesia refers to insensitivity to pain without loss of consciousness.
Neurotransmitter	A neurotransmitter is a chemical that is used to relay, amplify and modulate electrical signals between a neurons and another cell.
Endorphin	An endorphin is an endogenous opioid biochemical compound. They are peptides produced by the pituitary gland and the hypothalamus, and they resemble the opiates in their abilities to produce analgesia and a sense of well-being. In other words, they work as "natural pain killers."
Immune response	The body's defensive reaction to invasion by bacteria, viral agents, or other foreign substances is called the immune response.
Lymphocyte	A lymphocyte is a type of white blood cell involved in the human body's immune system. There are two broad categories, namely T cells and B cells. The lymphocyte play an important and integral part of the body's defenses.
Antigen	An antigen is a molecule that stimulates the production of antibodies. Usually, it is a protein or a polysaccharide, but can be any type of molecule, including small molecules (haptens) coupled to a protein (carrier).
Deprivation	Deprivation, is the loss or withholding of normal stimulation, nutrition, comfort, love, and so forth; a condition of lacking. The level of stimulation is less than what is required.
Chronic	Chronic refers to a relatively long duration, usually more than a few months.
Depression	In everyday language depression refers to any downturn in mood, which may be relatively transitory and perhaps due to something trivial. This is differentiated from Clinical depression which is marked by symptoms that last two weeks or more and are so severe that they interfere with daily living.
Anxiety	Anxiety is a complex combination of the feeling of fear, apprehension and worry often accompanied by physical sensations such as palpitations, chest pain and/or shortness of breath.
Evolution	Commonly used to refer to gradual change, evolution is the change in the frequency of alleles within a population from one generation to the next. This change may be caused by different mechanisms, including natural selection, genetic drift, or changes in population (gene flow).
Evolutionary perspective	A perspective that focuses on how humans have evolved and adapted behaviors required for survival against various environmental pressures over the long course is called the evolutionary perspective.
Discrimination	In Learning theory, discrimination refers the ability to distinguish between a conditioned stimulus and other stimuli. It can be brought about by extensive training or differential reinforcement. In social terms, it is the denial of privileges to a person or a group on the basis of prejudice.
Aversive stimulus	A stimulus that elicits pain, fear, or avoidance is an aversive stimulus.

Go to Cram101.com for the Practice Tests for this Chapter.

Chapter 9. Emotions, Stress, and Health

Stimulus	A change in an environmental condition that elicits a response is a stimulus.
Control group	A group that does not receive the treatment effect in an experiment is referred to as the control group or sometimes as the comparison group.
Analogy	An analogy is a comparison between two different things, in order to highlight some form of similarity. Analogy is the cognitive process of transferring information from a particular subject to another particular subject.
Control subjects	Control subjects are participants in an experiment who do not receive the treatment effect but for whom all other conditions are held comparable to those of experimental subjects.
Metabolism	Metabolism is the biochemical modification of chemical compounds in living organisms and cells.
Reasoning	Reasoning is the act of using reason to derive a conclusion from certain premises. There are two main methods to reach a conclusion, deductive reasoning and inductive reasoning.
Information processing	Information processing is an approach to the goal of understanding human thinking. The essence of the approach is to see cognition as being essentially computational in nature, with mind being the software and the brain being the hardware.
Hardiness	A personality characteristic associated with a lower rate of stress-related illness, consisting of three components: commitment, challenge, and control is hardiness.
Self-esteem	Self-esteem refers to a person's subjective appraisal of himself or herself as intrinsically positive or negative to some degree.
Denial	Denial is a psychological defense mechanism in which a person faced with a fact that is uncomfortable or painful to accept rejects it instead, insisting that it is not true despite what may be overwhelming evidence.
Social support	Social Support is the physical and emotional comfort given by family, friends, co-workers and others. Research has identified three main types of social support: emotional, practical, sharing points of view.
Reciprocity	Reciprocity, in interpersonal attraction, is the tendency to return feelings and attitudes that are expressed about us.
Stages	Stages represent relatively discrete periods of time in which functioning is qualitatively different from functioning at other periods.
Primary appraisal	A primary appraisal is an evaluation of the significance of a potentially stressful event according to how it will affect one's well-being-whether it is perceived as irrelevant or as involving harm or loss, threat, or challenge.
Attitude	An enduring mental representation of a person, place, or thing that evokes an emotional response and related behavior is called attitude.
Emotion-focused coping	Lazarus' emotion-focused coping describes individuals' response to stress demonstrated in an emotional manner, especially using defensive methods.
Problem-focused coping	Lazarus' problem-focused coping is a strategy used by individuals who face their troubles and try to solve them.
Problem solving	An attempt to find an appropriate way of attaining a goal when the goal is not readily available is called problem solving.
Corticosteroid	The Corticosteroid is a class of steroid hormones that are produced in the adrenal cortex. They are involved in a wide range of physiologic systems such as stress response, immune response and regulation of inflammation, carbohydrate metabolism, protein catabolism, blood electrolyte levels, and behavior.

Chapter 9. Emotions, Stress, and Health

Feedback	Feedback refers to information returned to a person about the effects a response has had.
Personality	Personality refers to the pattern of enduring characteristics that differentiates a person, the patterns of behaviors that make each individual unique.
Ambivalence	The simultaneous holding of strong positive and negative emotional attitudes toward the same situation or person is called ambivalence.
Cardiovascular system	The human cardiovascular system comprises the blood, the heart, and a dual-circuit system of blood vessels that serve as conduits between the heart, the lungs, and the peripheral tissues of the body.
Catecholamines	Catecholamines are chemical compounds derived from the amino acid tyrosine that act as hormones or neurotransmitters. High catecholamine levels in blood are associated with stress.
Attachment	Attachment is the tendency to seek closeness to another person and feel secure when that person is present.
Anecdotal evidence	Anecdotal evidence is unreliable evidence based on personal experience that has not been empirically tested, and which is often used in an argument as if it had been scientifically or statistically proven. The person using anecdotal evidence may or may not be aware of the fact that, by doing so, they are generalizing.
Practical intelligence	Practical intelligence focuses on the ability to use, apply, implement, and put into practice.
Cognitive-experiential self-theory	Cognitive-experiential self-theory suggests that our efforts to understand the world around us involve two distinct modes of thought: intuitive thought and deliberate, rational thought.
Consciousness	The awareness of the sensations, thoughts, and feelings being experienced at a given moment is called consciousness.
Self-fulfilling prophecy	A self-fulfilling prophecy is a prediction that, in being made, actually causes itself to become true.
Withdrawal of love	Withdrawal of love is a disciplinary strategy that may involve ignoring, isolating, or showing dislike for a child.
Meditation	Meditation usually refers to a state in which the body is consciously relaxed and the mind is allowed to become calm and focused.
Biofeedback	Biofeedback is the process of measuring and quantifying an aspect of a subject's physiology, analyzing the data, and then feeding back the information to the subject in a form that allows the subject to enact physiological change.
Transcendental Meditation	The simplified form of meditation brought to the United States by the Maharishi Mahesh Yogi and used as a method for coping with stress is called transcendental meditation.
Insomnia	Insomnia is a sleep disorder characterized by an inability to sleep and/or to remain asleep for a reasonable period during the night.
Metabolic rate	Metabolic rate refers to the rate at which the body burns calories to produce energy.
Diastolic blood pressure	Blood pressure level when the heart is at rest or between heartbeats is called diastolic blood pressure.
Autonomic nervous system	A division of the peripheral nervous system, the autonomic nervous system, regulates glands and activities such as heartbeat, respiration, digestion, and dilation of the pupils. It is responsible for homeostasis, maintaining a relatively constant internal environment.
Operant	A simple form of learning in which an organism learns to engage in behavior because it is

Chapter 9. Emotions, Stress, and Health

Chapter 9. Emotions, Stress, and Health

Conditioning	reinforced is referred to as operant conditioning. The consequences of a behavior produce changes in the probability of the behavior's occurence.
Conditioning	Conditioning describes the process by which behaviors can be learned or modified through interaction with the environment.
Migraine	Migraine is a form of headache, usually very intense and disabling. It is a neurologic disease.
Trauma	Trauma refers to a severe physical injury or wound to the body caused by an external force, or a psychological shock having a lasting effect on mental life.
Suppression	Suppression is the defense mechanism where a memory is deliberately forgotten.
Illusion	An illusion is a distortion of a sensory perception.
T cells	T cells are a subset of lymphocytes that play a large role in the immune response. Some attack antigens directly while others help regulate the system.
Trait	An enduring personality characteristic that tends to lead to certain behaviors is called a trait. The term trait also means a genetically inherited feature of an organism.
Adaptation	Adaptation is a lowering of sensitivity to a stimulus following prolonged exposure to that stimulus. Behavioral adaptations are special ways a particular organism behaves to survive in its natural habitat.
Locus of control	The place to which an individual attributes control over the receiving of reinforcers -either inside or outside the self is referred to as locus of control.
Sensation seeking	A generalized preference for high or low levels of sensory stimulation is referred to as sensation seeking.
Sensation	Sensation is the first stage in the chain of biochemical and neurologic events that begins with the impinging of a stimulus upon the receptor cells of a sensory organ, which then leads to perception, the mental state that is reflected in statements like "I see a uniformly blue wall."
Social psychology	Social psychology is the study of the nature and causes of human social behavior, with an emphasis on how people think towards each other and how they relate to each other.
Alarm reaction	The first stage of the general adaptation syndrome, which is triggered by the impact of a stressor and characterized by sympathetic activity is called the alarm reaction.
Life expectancy	The number of years that will probably be lived by the average person born in a particular year is called life expectancy.
Behavioral model	Explanation of human behavior, including dysfunction, based on principles of learning and adaptation derived from experimental psychology is referred to as a behavioral model.
Neuroendocrine system	The network of neurons and glands that make and secrete hormones are referred to as the neuroendocrine system.
Nicotine	Nicotine is an organic compound, an alkaloid found naturally throughout the tobacco plant, with a high concentration in the leaves. It is a potent nerve poison and is included in many insecticides. In lower concentrations, the substance is a stimulant and is one of the main factors leading to the pleasure and habit-forming qualities of tobacco smoking.
Relaxation training	Relaxation training is an intervention technique used for tics. The person is taught to relax the muscles involved in the tics.
Cognition	The intellectual processes through which information is obtained, transformed, stored, retrieved, and otherwise used is cognition.

Chapter 9. Emotions, Stress, and Health

Cognitive appraisal	Lazarus' term for individuals' interpretation of events in their lives as threatening, harmful, or challenging and their determination of whether they have the resources to effectively cope with the events is referred to as cognitive appraisal.
Variance	The degree to which scores differ among individuals in a distribution of scores is the variance.
Thalamus	An area near the center of the brain involved in the relay of sensory information to the cortex and in the functions of sleep and attention is the thalamus.
Amygdala	Located in the brain's medial temporal lobe, the almond-shaped amygdala is believed to play a key role in the emotions. It forms part of the limbic system and is linked to both fear responses and pleasure. Its size is positively correlated with aggressive behavior across species.
Neocortex	The neocortex is part of the cerebral cortex which covers most of the surface of the cerebral hemispheres including the frontal, parietal, occipital, and temporal lobes. Often seen as the hallmark of human intelligence, the role of this structure in the brain appears to be involved in conscious thought, spatial reasoning, and sensory perception.
Placebo effect	The placebo effect is the phenomenon that a patient's symptoms can be alleviated by an otherwise ineffective treatment, apparently because the individual expects or believes that it will work.
Placebo	Placebo refers to a bogus treatment that has the appearance of being genuine.
Dispositional optimism	Dispositional optimism is a cognitive style involving expectations of positive outcomes.
Addiction	Addiction is an uncontrollable compulsion to repeat a behavior regardless of its consequences. Many drugs or behaviors can precipitate a pattern of conditions recognized as addiction, which include a craving for more of the drug or behavior, increased physiological tolerance to exposure, and withdrawal symptoms in the absence of the stimulus.

Chapter 10. Goal-Incongruent [Negative] Emotions

Emotion	An emotion is a mental states that arise spontaneously, rather than through conscious effort. They are often accompanied by physiological changes.
Affect	A subjective feeling or emotional tone often accompanied by bodily expressions noticeable to others is called affect.
Motivation	In psychology, motivation is the driving force (desire) behind all actions of an organism.
Anxiety	Anxiety is a complex combination of the feeling of fear, apprehension and worry often accompanied by physical sensations such as palpitations, chest pain and/or shortness of breath.
Punishment	Punishment is the addtion of a stimulus that reduces the frequency of a response, or the removal of a stimulus that results in a reduction of the response.
Social comparison	Social comparison theory is the idea that individuals learn about and assess themselves by comparison with other people. Research shows that individuals tend to lean more toward social comparisons in situations that are ambiguous.
Social support	Social Support is the physical and emotional comfort given by family, friends, co-workers and others. Research has identified three main types of social support: emotional, practical, sharing points of view.
Brain	The brain controls and coordinates most movement, behavior and homeostatic body functions such as heartbeat, blood pressure, fluid balance and body temperature. Functions of the brain are responsible for cognition, emotion, memory, motor learning and other sorts of learning. The brain is primarily made up of two types of cells: glia and neurons.
Stimulus	A change in an environmental condition that elicits a response is a stimulus.
Depression	In everyday language depression refers to any downturn in mood, which may be relatively transitory and perhaps due to something trivial. This is differentiated from Clinical depression which is marked by symptoms that last two weeks or more and are so severe that they interfere with daily living.
Trait	An enduring personality characteristic that tends to lead to certain behaviors is called a trait. The term trait also means a genetically inherited feature of an organism.
Antecedents	In behavior modification, events that typically precede the target response are called antecedents.
Theories	Theories are logically self-consistent models or frameworks describing the behavior of a certain natural or social phenomenon. They are broad explanations and predictions concerning phenomena of interest.
Suicide	Suicide behavior is rare in childhood but escalates in adolescence. The suicide rate increases in a linear fashion from adolescence through late adulthood.
Heritability	Heritability It is that proportion of the observed variation in a particular phenotype within a particular population, that can be attributed to the contribution of genotype. In other words: it measures the extent to which differences between individuals in a population are due their being different genetically.
Behavioral inhibition system	The behavioral inhibition system is a circuit in the limbic system that responds to threat signals by inhibiting activity and causing anxiety.
Behavioral inhibition	Physiological probes of children with behavioral inhibition show significantly higher measures of activity in the sympathetic nervous system and hypothalamic-pituitary axis than in non-inhibited children. Kagan postulates that anxiety-prone children are born with a lower firing threshold in amygdala and hypothalamic neurons. His work provides a robust model for

Chapter 10. Goal-Incongruent [Negative] Emotions

	predicting temperamental forerunners of anxiety disorders.
Locus coeruleus	The Locus coeruleus is a nucleus in the brain stem (inferior to the cerebellum in the caudal midbrain/rostral pons) apparently responsible for the physiological reactions involved in stress and panic.
Attention	Attention is the cognitive process of selectively concentrating on one thing while ignoring other things. Psychologists have labeled three types of attention: sustained attention, selective attention, and divided attention.
Antianxiety drugs	Drugs that can reduce a person's level of excitability while increasing feelings of well-being are called antianxiety drugs.
Population	Population refers to all members of a well-defined group of organisms, events, or things.
Benzodiazepines	The benzodiazepines are a class of drugs with hypnotic, anxiolytic, anticonvulsant, amnestic and muscle relaxant properties. Benzodiazepines are often used for short-term relief of severe, disabling anxiety or insomnia.
Neurotransmitter	A neurotransmitter is a chemical that is used to relay, amplify and modulate electrical signals between a neurons and another cell.
Receptor site	A location on the dendrite of a receiving neuron that is tailored to receive a specific neurotransmitter is a receptor site.
Receptor	A sensory receptor is a structure that recognizes a stimulus in the internal or external environment of an organism. In response to stimuli the sensory receptor initiates sensory transduction by creating graded potentials or action potentials in the same cell or in an adjacent one.
Neuron	The neuron is the primary cell of the nervous system. They are found in the brain, the spinal cord, in the nerves and ganglia of the peripheral nervous system. It is a specialized cell that conducts impulses through the nervous system and contains three major parts: cell body, dendrites, and an axon. It can have many dendrites but only one axon.
Central nervous system	The vertebrate central nervous system consists of the brain and spinal cord.
Nervous system	The body's electrochemical communication circuitry, made up of billions of neurons is a nervous system.
Negative reinforcer	Negative reinforcer is a reinforcer that when removed increases the frequency of an response.
Reinforcer	In operant conditioning, a reinforcer is any stimulus that increases the probability that a preceding behavior will occur again. In Classical Conditioning, the unconditioned stimulus (US) is the reinforcer.
Amygdala	Located in the brain's medial temporal lobe, the almond-shaped amygdala is believed to play a key role in the emotions. It forms part of the limbic system and is linked to both fear responses and pleasure. Its size is positively correlated with aggressive behavior across species.
Lobes	The four major sections of the cerebral cortex: frontal, parietal, temporal, and occipital are called lobes.
Temperament	Temperament refers to a basic, innate disposition to change behavior. The activity level is an important dimension of temperament.
Phobia	A persistent, irrational fear of an object, situation, or activity that the person feels compelled to avoid is referred to as a phobia.

Chapter 10. Goal-Incongruent [Negative] Emotions

Chapter 10. Goal-Incongruent [Negative] Emotions

Classical conditioning	Classical conditioning is a simple form of learning in which an organism comes to associate or anticipate events. A neutral stimulus comes to evoke the response usually evoked by a natural or unconditioned stimulus by being paired repeatedly with the unconditioned stimulus.
Conditioning	Conditioning describes the process by which behaviors can be learned or modified through interaction with the environment.
Claustrophobia	Claustrophobia is an anxiety disorder that involves the fear of enclosed or confined spaces. It may be accompanied by panic attacks in situations such as being in elevators, trains or aircraft.
Acrophobia	An irrational fear of high places is referred to as acrophobia.
Systematic desensitization	Systematic desensitization refers to Wolpe's behavioral fear-reduction technique in which a hierarchy of fear-evoking stimuli are presented while the person remains relaxed. The fear-evoking stimuli thereby become associated with muscle relaxation.
Desensitization	Desensitization refers to the type of sensory or behavioral adaptation in which we become less sensitive to constant stimuli.
Countercondi-ioning	The process of eliminating a classically conditioned response by pairing the CS with an unconditioned stimulus for a response that is stronger than the conditioned response and that cannot occur at the same time as the CR is called counterconditioning.
Learning	Learning is a relatively permanent change in behavior that results from experience. Thus, to attribute a behavioral change to learning, the change must be relatively permanent and must result from experience.
Anxiety disorder	Anxiety disorder is a blanket term covering several different forms of abnormal anxiety, fear, phobia and nervous condition, that come on suddenly and prevent pursuing normal daily routines.
Fight-or-flight	The fight-or-flight response, also called the "acute stress response", was first described by Walter Cannon. Animals react to threats with a general discharge of the sympathetic nervous system. In layman's terms, an animal has two options when faced with danger. They can either face the threat, or they can avoid the threat.
Sympathetic	The sympathetic nervous system activates what is often termed the "fight or flight response". It is an automatic regulation system, that is, one that operates without the intervention of conscious thought.
Perception	Perception is the process of acquiring, interpreting, selecting, and organizing sensory information.
Alarm reaction	The first stage of the general adaptation syndrome, which is triggered by the impact of a stressor and characterized by sympathetic activity is called the alarm reaction.
Hypothesis	A specific statement about behavior or mental processes that is testable through research is a hypothesis.
Panic attack	An attack of overwhelming anxiety, fear, or terror is called panic attack.
Fear response	In the Mowrer-Miller theory, a response to a threatening or noxious situation that is covert but that is assumed to function as a stimulus to produce measurable physiological changes in the body and observable overt behavior is referred to as the fear response.
Negative affectivity	Negative affectivity is a personality variable that refers to a tendency to experience negative emotions across many different situations.
Self-concept	Self-concept refers to domain-specific evaluations of the self where a domain may be academics, athletics, etc.

Chapter 10. Goal-Incongruent [Negative] Emotions

Ambiguous stimuli	Patterns that allow more than one perceptual organization are called ambiguous stimuli.
Positive relationship	Statistically, a positive relationship refers to a mathematical relationship in which increases in one measure are matched by increases in the other.
Mental set	The tendency to respond to a new problem with an approach that was used successfully with similar problems, is called mental set.
Control subjects	Control subjects are participants in an experiment who do not receive the treatment effect but for whom all other conditions are held comparable to those of experimental subjects.
Insanity	A legal status indicating that a person cannot be held responsible for his or her actions because of mental illness is called insanity.
Generalized anxiety disorder	Generalized anxiety disorder is an anxiety disorder that is characterized by uncontrollable worry about everyday things. The frequency, intensity, and duration of the worry are disproportionate to the actual source of worry, and such worry often interferes with daily functioning.
Individual differences	Individual differences psychology studies the ways in which individual people differ in their behavior. This is distinguished from other aspects of psychology in that although psychology is ostensibly a study of individuals, modern psychologists invariably study groups.
Self-esteem	Self-esteem refers to a person's subjective appraisal of himself or herself as intrinsically positive or negative to some degree.
Elaboration	The extensiveness of processing at any given level of memory is called elaboration. The use of elaboration changes developmentally. Adolescents are more likely to use elaboration spontaneously than children.
Variable	A variable refers to a measurable factor, characteristic, or attribute of an individual or a system.
Attitude	An enduring mental representation of a person, place, or thing that evokes an emotional response and related behavior is called attitude.
Unipolar depression	Unipolar depression refers to a term applied to the disorder of individuals who have experienced episodes of depression but not of mania. It is referred to as major depression in DSM-IV-TR.
Lithium	Lithium salts are used as mood stabilizing drugs primarily in the treatment of bipolar disorder, depression, and mania; but also in treating schizophrenia. Lithium is widely distributed in the central nervous system and interacts with a number of neurotransmitters and receptors, decreasing noradrenaline release and increasing serotonin synthesis.
Psychotherapy	Psychotherapy is a set of techniques based on psychological principles intended to improve mental health, emotional or behavioral issues.
Major depressive episode	A major depressive episode is a common and severe experience of depression. It includes feelings of worthlessness, disturbances in bodily activities such as sleep, loss of interest, and the inability to experience pleasure. It lasts for at least two weeks.
Hypersomnia	Hypersomnia is an excessive amount of sleepiness, resulting in an inability to stay awake. A person is considered to have hypersomnia if he or she sleeps more than 10 hours per day on a regular basis for at least two weeks.
Guilt	Guilt describes many concepts related to a negative emotion or condition caused by actions which are believed to be, morally wrong. According to Freud, the avoidance of guilt is the basis for moral behavior.

Chapter 10. Goal-Incongruent [Negative] Emotions

Suicidal ideation	Suicidal ideation refers to having serious thoughts about committing suicide.
Survey	A method of scientific investigation in which a large sample of people answer questions about their attitudes or behavior is referred to as a survey.
Individualism	Individualism refers to putting personal goals ahead of group goals and defining one's identity in terms of personal attributes rather than group memberships.
Autonomy	Autonomy is the condition of something that does not depend on anything else.
Basic emotions	Basic emotions are those found in all cultures, as evidenced by the same facial expressions. They include: fear, anger, disgust, surprise, happiness, and distress.
Identical twins	Identical twins occur when a single egg is fertilized to form one zygote (monozygotic) but the zygote then divides into two separate embryos. The two embryos develop into foetuses sharing the same womb. Monozygotic twins are genetically identical unless there has been a mutation in development, and they are almost always the same gender.
Depressive disorders	Depressive disorders are mood disorders in which the individual suffers depression without ever experiencing mania.
Fraternal twins	Fraternal twins usually occur when two fertilized eggs are implanted in the uterine wall at the same time. The two eggs form two zygotes, and these twins are therefore also known as dizygotic. Dizygotic twins are no more similar genetically than any siblings.
Family studies	Scientific studies in which researchers assess hereditary influence by examining blood relatives to see how much they resemble each other on a specific trait are called family studies.
Cognition	The intellectual processes through which information is obtained, transformed, stored, retrieved, and otherwise used is cognition.
Right hemisphere	The brain is divided into left and right cerebral hemispheres. The right hemisphere of the cortex controls the left side of the body.
Chronic	Chronic refers to a relatively long duration, usually more than a few months.
Catecholamines	Catecholamines are chemical compounds derived from the amino acid tyrosine that act as hormones or neurotransmitters. High catecholamine levels in blood are associated with stress.
Catecholamine hypothesis	The Catecholamine hypothesis is an outdated, simplistic theory of mood disorder etiology stating that norepinephrine excess causes mania, and that low levels of it cause some forms of depression.
Norepinephrine	Norepinephrine is released from the adrenal glands as a hormone into the blood, but it is also a neurotransmitter in the nervous system. As a stress hormone, it affects parts of the human brain where attention and impulsivity are controlled. Along with epinephrine, this compound effects the fight-or-flight response, activating the sympathetic nervous system to directly increase heart rate, release energy from fat, and increase muscle readiness.
Dopamine	Dopamine is critical to the way the brain controls our movements and is a crucial part of the basal ganglia motor loop. It is commonly associated with the 'pleasure system' of the brain, providing feelings of enjoyment and reinforcement to motivate us to do, or continue doing, certain activities.
Serotonin	Serotonin, a neurotransmitter, is believed to play an important part of the biochemistry of depression, bipolar disorder and anxiety. It is also believed to be influential on sexuality and appetite.
Species	Species refers to a reproductively isolated breeding population.

Go to **Cram101.com** for the Practice Tests for this Chapter.

Chapter 10. Goal-Incongruent [Negative] Emotions

Incentive	An incentive is what is expected once a behavior is performed. An incentive acts as a reinforcer.
Adaptive behavior	An adaptive behavior increases the probability of the individual or organism to survive or exist within its environment.
Gene	A gene is an ultramicroscopic area of the chromosome. It is the smallest physical unit of the DNA molecule that carries a piece of hereditary information.
Attachment	Attachment is the tendency to seek closeness to another person and feel secure when that person is present.
Social motives	Social motives refer to drives acquired through experience and interaction with others.
Motives	Needs or desires that energize and direct behavior toward a goal are motives.
Cognitive therapy	Cognitive therapy is a kind of psychotherapy used to treat depression, anxiety disorders, phobias, and other forms of mental disorder. It involves recognizing distorted thinking and learning how to replace it with more realistic thoughts and actions.
Tricyclic antidepressant	A tricyclic antidepressant is of a class of antidepressant drugs first used in the 1950s. They are named after the drugs' molecular structure, which contains three rings of atoms.
Antidepressant	An antidepressant is a medication used primarily in the treatment of clinical depression. They are not thought to produce tolerance, although sudden withdrawal may produce adverse effects. They create little if any immediate change in mood and require between several days and several weeks to take effect.
Tricyclic	Tricyclic antidepressants are a class of antidepressant drugs first used in the 1950s. They are named after the drugs' molecular structure, which contains three rings of atoms.
Antidepressants	Antidepressants are medications used primarily in the treatment of clinical depression. Antidepressants create little if any immediate change in mood and require between several days and several weeks to take effect.
Cocaine	Cocaine is a crystalline tropane alkaloid that is obtained from the leaves of the coca plant. It is a stimulant of the central nervous system and an appetite suppressant, creating what has been described as a euphoric sense of happiness and increased energy.
Reuptake	Reuptake is the reabsorption of a neurotransmitter by the molecular transporter of a pre-synaptic neuron after it has performed its function of transmitting a neural impulse.
Monoamine oxidase inhibitors	Monoamine oxidase inhibitors are a group of antidepressant drugs that prevent the enzyme monoamine oxidase from deactivating neurotransmitters of the central nervous system.
Monoamine oxidase	Monoamine oxidase is an enzyme that catalyzes the oxidation of monoamines. They are found bound to the outer membrane of mitochondria in most cell types in the body. Because of the vital role that it play in the inactivation of neurotransmitters, dysfunction (too much/too little MAO activity) is thought to be responsible for a number of neurological disorders.
Enzyme	An enzyme is a protein that catalyzes, or speeds up, a chemical reaction. Enzymes are essential to sustain life because most chemical reactions in biological cells would occur too slowly, or would lead to different products, without enzymes.
Obsessive-compulsive disorder	Obsessive-compulsive disorder is an anxiety disorder manifested in a variety of forms, but is most commonly characterized by a subject's obsessive drive to perform a particular task or set of tasks, compulsions commonly termed rituals.
Instrumental learning	Operant conditioning, sometimes called instrumental learning, was first extensively studied by Thorndike. In instrumental learning, the organism must act in a certain way before it is

Chapter 10. Goal-Incongruent [Negative] Emotions

	reinforced; that is, reinforcement is contingent on the organism's behavior.
Learned helplessness	Learned helplessness is a description of the effect of inescapable positive punishment (such as electrical shock) on animal (and by extension, human) behavior.
Personality	Personality refers to the pattern of enduring characteristics that differentiates a person, the patterns of behaviors that make each individual unique.
Personality inventory	A self-report questionnaire by which an examinee indicates whether statements assessing habitual tendencies apply to him or her is referred to as a personality inventory.
Construct	A generalized concept, such as anxiety or gravity, is a construct.
Proactive interference	Proactive interference occurs when information learned earlier disrupts the recall of material learned later. This can become a problem when new information cannot be used correctly as it is interfered with by the older information.
Validity	The extent to which a test measures what it is intended to measure is called validity.
Learned helplessness theory	Learned helplessness theory of personality suggests that individuals acquire passivity, a sense of being unable to act and to control their lives. Often, this happens through unpleasant experiences and traumas against which their efforts were ineffective.
Stroke	A stroke occurs when the blood supply to a part of the brain is suddenly interrupted by occlusion, by hemorrhage, or other causes
Diastolic blood pressure	Blood pressure level when the heart is at rest or between heartbeats is called diastolic blood pressure.
Deprivation	Deprivation, is the loss or withholding of normal stimulation, nutrition, comfort, love, and so forth; a condition of lacking. The level of stimulation is less than what is required.
Schema	Schema refers to a way of mentally representing the world, such as a belief or an expectation, that can influence perception of persons, objects, and situations.
Conformity	Conformity is the degree to which members of a group will change their behavior, views and attitudes to fit the views of the group. The group can influence members via unconscious processes or via overt social pressure on individuals.
Aversive stimulus	A stimulus that elicits pain, fear, or avoidance is an aversive stimulus.
Empirical	Empirical means the use of working hypotheses which are capable of being disproved using observation or experiment.
Sexual abuse	Sexual abuse is a term used to describe non- consentual sexual relations between two or more parties which are considered criminally and/or morally offensive.
Rape	Rape is a crime where the victim is forced into sexual activity, in particular sexual penetration, against his or her will.
Eating disorders	Psychological disorders characterized by distortion of the body image and gross disturbances in eating patterns are called eating disorders.
Alcoholism	A disorder that involves long-term, repeated, uncontrolled, compulsive, and excessive use of alcoholic beverages and that impairs the drinker's health and work and social relationships is called alcoholism.
Empathy	Empathy is the recognition and understanding of the states of mind, including beliefs, desires and particularly emotions of others without injecting your own.
Altruism	Altruism is being helpful to other people with little or no interest in being rewarded for one's efforts. This is distinct from merely helping others.

Chapter 10. Goal-Incongruent [Negative] Emotions

Chapter 10. Goal-Incongruent [Negative] Emotions

Goal-directed behavior	Goal-directed behavior is means-end problem solving behavior. In the infant, such behavior is first observed in the latter part of the first year.
Evolutionary perspective	A perspective that focuses on how humans have evolved and adapted behaviors required for survival against various environmental pressures over the long course is called the evolutionary perspective.
Evolution	Commonly used to refer to gradual change, evolution is the change in the frequency of alleles within a population from one generation to the next. This change may be caused by different mechanisms, including natural selection, genetic drift, or changes in population (gene flow).
Extinction	In operant extinction, if no reinforcement is delivered after the response, gradually the behavior will no longer occur in the presence of the stimulus. The process is more rapid following continuous reinforcement rather than after partial reinforcement. In Classical Conditioning, repeated presentations of the CS without being followed by the US results in the extinction of the CS.
Discrimination	In Learning theory, discrimination refers the ability to distinguish between a conditioned stimulus and other stimuli. It can be brought about by extensive training or differential reinforcement. In social terms, it is the denial of privileges to a person or a group on the basis of prejudice.
Generalization	In conditioning, the tendency for a conditioned response to be evoked by stimuli that are similar to the stimulus to which the response was conditioned is a generalization. The greater the similarity among the stimuli, the greater the probability of generalization.
Social learning	Social learning is learning that occurs as a function of observing, retaining and replicating behavior observed in others. Although social learning can occur at any stage in life, it is thought to be particularly important during childhood, particularly as authority becomes important.
Power assertion	A discipline technique in which a parent attempts to gain control over a child or a child's resources is called power assertion.
Moral development	Development regarding rules and conventions about what people should do in their interactions with other people is called moral development.
Love withdrawal	A discipline technique in which a parent removes attention or love from a child is referred to as love withdrawal.
Norms	In testing, standards of test performance that permit the comparison of one person's score on the test to the scores of others who have taken the same test are referred to as norms.
Socialization	Social rules and social relations are created, communicated, and changed in verbal and nonverbal ways creating social complexity useful in identifying outsiders and intelligent breeding partners. The process of learning these skills is called socialization.
Self-reflection	In Bandura's social cognitive theory, the ability to analyze one's thoughts and actions is referred to as self-reflection.
Need for achievement	Need for Achievement is a term introduced by David McClelland into the field of psychology, referring to an individual's desire for significant accomplishment, mastering of skills, control, or high standards.

Chapter 10. Goal-Incongruent [Negative] Emotions

Chapter 11. Goal-Congruent [Positive] Emotions

Emotion	An emotion is a mental states that arise spontaneously, rather than through conscious effort. They are often accompanied by physiological changes.
Survey	A method of scientific investigation in which a large sample of people answer questions about their attitudes or behavior is referred to as a survey.
Affect	A subjective feeling or emotional tone often accompanied by bodily expressions noticeable to others is called affect.
Life satisfaction	A person's attitudes about his or her overall life are referred to as life satisfaction.
Norms	In testing, standards of test performance that permit the comparison of one person's score on the test to the scores of others who have taken the same test are referred to as norms.
Positive correlation	A relationship between two variables in which both vary in the same direction is called a positive correlation.
Correlation	A statistical technique for determining the degree of association between two or more variables is referred to as correlation.
Variance	The degree to which scores differ among individuals in a distribution of scores is the variance.
Heritability	Heritability It is that proportion of the observed variation in a particular phenotype within a particular population, that can be attributed to the contribution of genotype. In other words: it measures the extent to which differences between individuals in a population are due their being different genetically.
Personality trait	According to the Diagnostic and Statistical Manual of the American Psychiatric Association, a personality trait is a "prominent aspect of personality that is exhibited in a wide range of important social and personal contexts. ...".
Personality	Personality refers to the pattern of enduring characteristics that differentiates a person, the patterns of behaviors that make each individual unique.
Trait	An enduring personality characteristic that tends to lead to certain behaviors is called a trait. The term trait also means a genetically inherited feature of an organism.
Extraversion	Extraversion, one of the big-five personailty traits, is marked by pronounced engagement with the external world. They are people who enjoy being with people, are full of energy, and often experience positive emotions.
Neuroticism	Eysenck's use of the term neuroticism (or Emotional Stability) was proposed as the dimension describing individual differences in the predisposition towards neurotic disorder.
Behavioral inhibition system	The behavioral inhibition system is a circuit in the limbic system that responds to threat signals by inhibiting activity and causing anxiety.
Behavioral inhibition	Physiological probes of children with behavioral inhibition show significantly higher measures of activity in the sympathetic nervous system and hypothalamic-pituitary axis than in non-inhibited children. Kagan postulates that anxiety-prone children are born with a lower firing threshold in amygdala and hypothalamic neurons. His work provides a robust model for predicting temperamental forerunners of anxiety disorders.
Punishment	Punishment is the addtion of a stimulus that reduces the frequency of a response, or the removal of a stimulus that results in a reduction of the response.
Left hemisphere	The left hemisphere of the cortex controls the right side of the body, coordinates complex movements, and, in 95% of people, controls the production of speech and written language.

Go to **Cram101.com** for the Practice Tests for this Chapter.

Chapter 11. Goal-Congruent [Positive] Emotions

Chapter 11. Goal-Congruent [Positive] Emotions

Right hemisphere	The brain is divided into left and right cerebral hemispheres. The right hemisphere of the cortex controls the left side of the body.
Gene	A gene is an ultramicroscopic area of the chromosome. It is the smallest physical unit of the DNA molecule that carries a piece of hereditary information.
Brain	The brain controls and coordinates most movement, behavior and homeostatic body functions such as heartbeat, blood pressure, fluid balance and body temperature. Functions of the brain are responsible for cognition, emotion, memory, motor learning and other sorts of learning. The brain is primarily made up of two types of cells: glia and neurons.
Learning	Learning is a relatively permanent change in behavior that results from experience. Thus, to attribute a behavioral change to learning, the change must be relatively permanent and must result from experience.
Cognition	The intellectual processes through which information is obtained, transformed, stored, retrieved, and otherwise used is cognition.
Neuroscience	A field that combines the work of psychologists, biologists, biochemists, medical researchers, and others in the study of the structure and function of the nervous system is neuroscience.
Evolutionary perspective	A perspective that focuses on how humans have evolved and adapted behaviors required for survival against various environmental pressures over the long course is called the evolutionary perspective.
Genetics	Genetics is the science of genes, heredity, and the variation of organisms.
Evolution	Commonly used to refer to gradual change, evolution is the change in the frequency of alleles within a population from one generation to the next. This change may be caused by different mechanisms, including natural selection, genetic drift, or changes in population (gene flow).
Amygdala	Located in the brain's medial temporal lobe, the almond-shaped amygdala is believed to play a key role in the emotions. It forms part of the limbic system and is linked to both fear responses and pleasure. Its size is positively correlated with aggressive behavior across species.
Launching	The process in which youths move into adulthood and exit their family of origin is called launching. It can be a time to formulate life goals, to develop an identity, and to become more independent before joining with another person to form a new family.
Blocking	If the one of the two members of a compound stimulus fails to produce the CR due to an earlier conditioning of the other member of the compound stimulus, blocking has occurred.
Incentive	An incentive is what is expected once a behavior is performed. An incentive acts as a reinforcer.
Motivation	In psychology, motivation is the driving force (desire) behind all actions of an organism.
Altruism	Altruism is being helpful to other people with little or no interest in being rewarded for one's efforts. This is distinct from merely helping others.
Extrinsic motivation	Responding to external incentives such as rewards and punishments is form of extrinsic motivation. Traditionally, extrinsic motivation has been used to motivate employees: Payments, rewards, control, or punishments.
Intrinsic motivation	Intrinsic motivation causes people to engage in an activity for its own sake. They are subjective factors and include self-determination, curiosity, challenge, effort, and others.
Attention	Attention is the cognitive process of selectively concentrating on one thing while ignoring other things. Psychologists have labeled three types of attention: sustained attention,

Chapter 11. Goal-Congruent [Positive] Emotions

Chapter 11. Goal-Congruent [Positive] Emotions

	selective attention, and divided attention.
Feedback	Feedback refers to information returned to a person about the effects a response has had.
Anxiety	Anxiety is a complex combination of the feeling of fear, apprehension and worry often accompanied by physical sensations such as palpitations, chest pain and/or shortness of breath.
Ego	In Freud's view the Ego serves to balance our primitive needs and our moral beliefs and taboos. Relying on experience, a healthy Ego provides the ability to adapt to reality and interact with the outside world.
Self-esteem	Self-esteem refers to a person's subjective appraisal of himself or herself as intrinsically positive or negative to some degree.
Paradigm	Paradigm refers to the set of practices that defines a scientific discipline during a particular period of time. It provides a framework from which to conduct research, it ensures that a certain range of phenomena, those on which the paradigm focuses, are explored thoroughly. Itmay also blind scientists to other, perhaps more fruitful, ways of dealing with their subject matter.
Catecholamines	Catecholamines are chemical compounds derived from the amino acid tyrosine that act as hormones or neurotransmitters. High catecholamine levels in blood are associated with stress.
Epinephrine	Epinephrine is a hormone and a neurotransmitter. Epinephrine plays a central role in the short-term stress reaction—the physiological response to threatening or exciting conditions. It is secreted by the adrenal medulla. When released into the bloodstream, epinephrine binds to multiple receptors and has numerous effects throughout the body.
Norepinephrine	Norepinephrine is released from the adrenal glands as a hormone into the blood, but it is also a neurotransmitter in the nervous system. As a stress hormone, it affects parts of the human brain where attention and impulsivity are controlled. Along with epinephrine, this compound effects the fight-or-flight response, activating the sympathetic nervous system to directly increase heart rate, release energy from fat, and increase muscle readiness.
Adaptive behavior	An adaptive behavior increases the probability of the individual or organism to survive or exist within its environment.
Self-efficacy	Self-efficacy is the belief that one has the capabilities to execute the courses of actions required to manage prospective situations.
Avoidance learning	Avoidance learning describes how a learner develops a pattern that will allow him/her to avoid an aversive location or situation. Avoidance learning takes place when a map is created which allows the learner not to go to the place where the aversive is.
Learned helplessness	Learned helplessness is a description of the effect of inescapable positive punishment (such as electrical shock) on animal (and by extension, human) behavior.
Guilt	Guilt describes many concepts related to a negative emotion or condition caused by actions which are believed to be, morally wrong. According to Freud, the avoidance of guilt is the basis for moral behavior.
Learning paradigm	In abnormal psychology, the set of assumptions that abnormal behavior is learned in the same way as other human behavior is a learning paradigm.
Positive relationship	Statistically, a positive relationship refers to a mathematical relationship in which increases in one measure are matched by increases in the other.
Acquisition	Acquisition is the process of adapting to the environment, learning or becoming conditioned. In classical conditoning terms, it is the initial learning of the stimulus response link, which involves a neutral stimulus being associated with a unconditioned stimulus and becoming

Chapter 11. Goal-Congruent [Positive] Emotions

Chapter 11. Goal-Congruent [Positive] Emotions

	a conditioned stimulus.
Self-efficacy theory	Self-efficacy theory is a motivation theory based on the idea that people perform well when they believe they are capable of doing the job.
Agoraphobia	An irrational fear of open, crowded places is called agoraphobia. Many people suffering from agoraphobia, however, are not afraid of the open spaces themselves, but of situations often associated with these spaces, such as social gatherings.
Panic attack	An attack of overwhelming anxiety, fear, or terror is called panic attack.
Strange situation	An observational measure of infant attachment that requires the infant to move through a series of introductions, separations, and reunions with the caregiver and an adult stranger in a prescribed order is called Ainsworth's strange situation.
Amphetamine	Amphetamine is a synthetic stimulant used to suppress the appetite, control weight, and treat disorders including narcolepsy and ADHD. It is also used recreationally and for performance enhancement.
Aversive stimulus	A stimulus that elicits pain, fear, or avoidance is an aversive stimulus.
Stimulus	A change in an environmental condition that elicits a response is a stimulus.
Variable	A variable refers to a measurable factor, characteristic, or attribute of an individual or a system.
Self-concept	Self-concept refers to domain-specific evaluations of the self where a domain may be academics, athletics, etc.
Attitude	An enduring mental representation of a person, place, or thing that evokes an emotional response and related behavior is called attitude.
Goal-directed behavior	Goal-directed behavior is means-end problem solving behavior. In the infant, such behavior is first observed in the latter part of the first year.
Endorphin	An endorphin is an endogenous opioid biochemical compound. They are peptides produced by the pituitary gland and the hypothalamus, and they resemble the opiates in their abilities to produce analgesia and a sense of well-being. In other words, they work as "natural pain killers."
Serotonin	Serotonin, a neurotransmitter, is believed to play an important part of the biochemistry of depression, bipolar disorder and anxiety. It is also believed to be influential on sexuality and appetite.
Control group	A group that does not receive the treatment effect in an experiment is referred to as the control group or sometimes as the comparison group.
Questionnaire	A self-report method of data collection or clinical assessment method in which the individual being studied checks off items on a printed list, answers multiple-choice questions, or writes out answers to essay questions aimed at producing a selfdescription is called questionnaire.
Longitudinal study	Longitudinal study is a type of developmental study in which the same group of participants is followed and measured for an extended period of time, often years.
Depression	In everyday language depression refers to any downturn in mood, which may be relatively transitory and perhaps due to something trivial. This is differentiated from Clinical depression which is marked by symptoms that last two weeks or more and are so severe that they interfere with daily living.
Aptitude test	A test designed to predict a person's ability in a particular area or line of work is called

Chapter 11. Goal-Congruent [Positive] Emotions

Chapter 11. Goal-Congruent [Positive] Emotions

	an aptitude test.
Mental processes	The thoughts, feelings, and motives that each of us experiences privately but that cannot be observed directly are called mental processes.
Tumor	A tumor is an abnormal growth that when located in the brain can either be malignant and directly destroy brain tissue, or be benign and disrupt functioning by increasing intracranial pressure.
Immune system	The most important function of the human immune system occurs at the cellular level of the blood and tissues. The lymphatic and blood circulation systems are highways for specialized white blood cells. These cells include B cells, T cells, natural killer cells, and macrophages. All function with the primary objective of recognizing, attacking and destroying bacteria, viruses, cancer cells, and all substances seen as foreign.
Immune response	The body's defensive reaction to invasion by bacteria, viral agents, or other foreign substances is called the immune response.
Primary appraisal	A primary appraisal is an evaluation of the significance of a potentially stressful event according to how it will affect one's well-being-whether it is perceived as irrelevant or as involving harm or loss, threat, or challenge.
Individualism	Individualism refers to putting personal goals ahead of group goals and defining one's identity in terms of personal attributes rather than group memberships.
Negative feedback	In negative feedback, the output of a system is added back into the input, so as to reverse the direction of change. This tends to keep the output from changing, so it is stabilizing and attempts to maintain homeostasis.
Attachment	Attachment is the tendency to seek closeness to another person and feel secure when that person is present.
Adolescence	The period of life bounded by puberty and the assumption of adult responsibilities is adolescence.
Social motives	Social motives refer to drives acquired through experience and interaction with others.
Motives	Needs or desires that energize and direct behavior toward a goal are motives.
Attachment style	Attachment style refers to the way a person typically interacts with significant others.
Prototype	A concept of a category of objects or events that serves as a good example of the category is called a prototype.
Job satisfaction	A person's attitudes and feelings about his or her job and facets of the job is called job satisfaction.
Avoidant attachment	A type of insecure attachment characterized by apparent indifference to the leave-takings of, and reunions with, an attachment figure is referred to as avoidant attachment.
Secure attachment	With secure attachment, the infant uses a caregiver as a secure base from which to explore the environment. Ainsworth believes that secure attachment in the first year of life provides an important foundation for psychological development later in life.
Social support	Social Support is the physical and emotional comfort given by family, friends, co-workers and others. Research has identified three main types of social support: emotional, practical, sharing points of view.
Locus of control	The place to which an individual attributes control over the receiving of reinforcers -either inside or outside the self is referred to as locus of control.
Neurosis	Neurosis, any mental disorder that, although may cause distress, does not interfere with

Go to Cram101.com for the Practice Tests for this Chapter.

Chapter 11. Goal-Congruent [Positive] Emotions

Chapter 11. Goal-Congruent [Positive] Emotions

	rational thought or the persons' ability to function.
Empirical	Empirical means the use of working hypotheses which are capable of being disproved using observation or experiment.
Ambivalent attachment	Ambivalent attachment refers to an insecure attachment category in which adolescents are hyper-tuned to attachment experiences. This is thought to mainly occur because parents are inconsistently available to the adolescents.

Chapter 11. Goal-Congruent [Positive] Emotions

Chapter 12. From Curiosity to Creativity

Learning	Learning is a relatively permanent change in behavior that results from experience. Thus, to attribute a behavioral change to learning, the change must be relatively permanent and must result from experience.
Sensation seeking	A generalized preference for high or low levels of sensory stimulation is referred to as sensation seeking.
Sensation	Sensation is the first stage in the chain of biochemical and neurologic events that begins with the impinging of a stimulus upon the receptor cells of a sensory organ, which then leads to perception, the mental state that is reflected in statements like "I see a uniformly blue wall."
Anxiety	Anxiety is a complex combination of the feeling of fear, apprehension and worry often accompanied by physical sensations such as palpitations, chest pain and/or shortness of breath.
Attitude	An enduring mental representation of a person, place, or thing that evokes an emotional response and related behavior is called attitude.
Self-esteem	Self-esteem refers to a person's subjective appraisal of himself or herself as intrinsically positive or negative to some degree.
Motivation	In psychology, motivation is the driving force (desire) behind all actions of an organism.
Creativity	Creativity is the ability to think about something in novel and unusual ways and come up with unique solutions to problems. It involves divergent thinking, having many solutions or views to a problem.
Personality	Personality refers to the pattern of enduring characteristics that differentiates a person, the patterns of behaviors that make each individual unique.
Primary drive	A primary drive is a state of tension or arousal arising from a biological or innate need; it is one not based on learning. A primary drive activates behavior.
Reinforcement	In operant conditioning, reinforcement is any change in an environment that (a) occurs after the behavior, (b) seems to make that behavior re-occur more often in the future and (c) that reoccurence of behavior must be the result of the change.
Stimulus	A change in an environmental condition that elicits a response is a stimulus.
Prototype	A concept of a category of objects or events that serves as a good example of the category is called a prototype.
Theories	Theories are logically self-consistent models or frameworks describing the behavior of a certain natural or social phenomenon. They are broad explanations and predictions concerning phenomena of interest.
Adaptation	Adaptation is a lowering of sensitivity to a stimulus following prolonged exposure to that stimulus. Behavioral adaptations are special ways a particular organism behaves to survive in its natural habitat.
Evolutionary perspective	A perspective that focuses on how humans have evolved and adapted behaviors required for survival against various environmental pressures over the long course is called the evolutionary perspective.
Affect	A subjective feeling or emotional tone often accompanied by bodily expressions noticeable to others is called affect.
Feedback loop	A system in which the hypothalamus, pituitary gland, and gonads regulate each other's functioning through a series of hormonal messages is a feedback loop.
Feedback	Feedback refers to information returned to a person about the effects a response has had.

Go to **Cram101.com** for the Practice Tests for this Chapter.

Chapter 12. From Curiosity to Creativity

Chapter 12. From Curiosity to Creativity

Social skills	Social skills are skills used to interact and communicate with others to assist status in the social structure and other motivations.
Amphetamine	Amphetamine is a synthetic stimulant used to suppress the appetite, control weight, and treat disorders including narcolepsy and ADHD. It is also used recreationally and for performance enhancement.
Attention	Attention is the cognitive process of selectively concentrating on one thing while ignoring other things. Psychologists have labeled three types of attention: sustained attention, selective attention, and divided attention.
Extraversion	Extraversion, one of the big-five personailty traits, is marked by pronounced engagement with the external world. They are people who enjoy being with people, are full of energy, and often experience positive emotions.
Motives	Needs or desires that energize and direct behavior toward a goal are motives.
Behavioral inhibition system	The behavioral inhibition system is a circuit in the limbic system that responds to threat signals by inhibiting activity and causing anxiety.
Behavioral inhibition	Physiological probes of children with behavioral inhibition show significantly higher measures of activity in the sympathetic nervous system and hypothalamic-pituitary axis than in non-inhibited children. Kagan postulates that anxiety-prone children are born with a lower firing threshold in amygdala and hypothalamic neurons. His work provides a robust model for predicting temperamental forerunners of anxiety disorders.
Subjective experience	Subjective experience refers to reality as it is perceived and interpreted, not as it exists objectively.
Information processing	Information processing is an approach to the goal of understanding human thinking. The essence of the approach is to see cognition as being essentially computational in nature, with mind being the software and the brain being the hardware.
Hypothesis	A specific statement about behavior or mental processes that is testable through research is a hypothesis.
Intrinsic motivation	Intrinsic motivation causes people to engage in an activity for its own sake. They are subjective factors and include self-determination, curiosity, challenge, effort, and others.
Autonomy	Autonomy is the condition of something that does not depend on anything else.
Locus of control	The place to which an individual attributes control over the receiving of reinforcers -either inside or outside the self is referred to as locus of control.
Construct	A generalized concept, such as anxiety or gravity, is a construct.
Meta-analysis	In statistics, a meta-analysis combines the results of several studies that address a set of related research hypotheses.
Internalization	The developmental change from behavior that is externally controlled to behavior that is controlled by internal standards and principles is referred to as internalization.
Social motives	Social motives refer to drives acquired through experience and interaction with others.
Tactile	Pertaining to the sense of touch is referred to as tactile.
Sensory deprivation	Sensory deprivation is the deliberate reduction or removal of stimuli from one or more of the senses. Though short periods of sensory deprivation can be relaxing, extended deprivation can result in extreme anxiety, hallucinations, bizarre thoughts, depression, and antisocial behavior.

Chapter 12. From Curiosity to Creativity

Chapter 12. From Curiosity to Creativity

Deprivation	Deprivation, is the loss or withholding of normal stimulation, nutrition, comfort, love, and so forth; a condition of lacking. The level of stimulation is less than what is required.
Personality type	A persistent style of complex behaviors defined by a group of related traits is referred to as a personality type. Myer Friedman and his co-workers first defined personality types in the 1950s. Friedman classified people into 2 categories, Type A and Type B.
Questionnaire	A self-report method of data collection or clinical assessment method in which the individual being studied checks off items on a printed list, answers multiple-choice questions, or writes out answers to essay questions aimed at producing a selfdescription is called questionnaire.
Trait	An enduring personality characteristic that tends to lead to certain behaviors is called a trait. The term trait also means a genetically inherited feature of an organism.
Monoamine oxidase	Monoamine oxidase is an enzyme that catalyzes the oxidation of monoamines. They are found bound to the outer membrane of mitochondria in most cell types in the body. Because of the vital role that it play in the inactivation of neurotransmitters, dysfunction (too much/too little MAO activity) is thought to be responsible for a number of neurological disorders.
Enzyme	An enzyme is a protein that catalyzes, or speeds up, a chemical reaction. Enzymes are essential to sustain life because most chemical reactions in biological cells would occur too slowly, or would lead to different products, without enzymes.
Neurotransmitter	A neurotransmitter is a chemical that is used to relay, amplify and modulate electrical signals between a neurons and another cell.
Norepinephrine	Norepinephrine is released from the adrenal glands as a hormone into the blood, but it is also a neurotransmitter in the nervous system. As a stress hormone, it affects parts of the human brain where attention and impulsivity are controlled. Along with epinephrine, this compound effects the fight-or-flight response, activating the sympathetic nervous system to directly increase heart rate, release energy from fat, and increase muscle readiness.
Dopamine	Dopamine is critical to the way the brain controls our movements and is a crucial part of the basal ganglia motor loop. It is commonly associated with the 'pleasure system' of the brain, providing feelings of enjoyment and reinforcement to motivate us to do, or continue doing, certain activities.
Serotonin	Serotonin, a neurotransmitter, is believed to play an important part of the biochemistry of depression, bipolar disorder and anxiety. It is also believed to be influential on sexuality and appetite.
Brain	The brain controls and coordinates most movement, behavior and homeostatic body functions such as heartbeat, blood pressure, fluid balance and body temperature. Functions of the brain are responsible for cognition, emotion, memory, motor learning and other sorts of learning. The brain is primarily made up of two types of cells: glia and neurons.
Cocaine	Cocaine is a crystalline tropane alkaloid that is obtained from the leaves of the coca plant. It is a stimulant of the central nervous system and an appetite suppressant, creating what has been described as a euphoric sense of happiness and increased energy.
Genetics	Genetics is the science of genes, heredity, and the variation of organisms.
Testosterone	Testosterone is a steroid hormone from the androgen group. It is the principal male sex hormone and the "original" anabolic steroid.
Cognition	The intellectual processes through which information is obtained, transformed, stored, retrieved, and otherwise used is cognition.
Punishment	Punishment is the addtion of a stimulus that reduces the frequency of a response, or the

Chapter 12. From Curiosity to Creativity

Chapter 12. From Curiosity to Creativity

	removal of a stimulus that results in a reduction of the response.
Marijuana	Marijuana is the dried vegetable matter of the Cannabis sativa plant. It contains large concentrations of compounds that have medicinal and psychoactive effects when consumed, usually by smoking or eating.
Disinhibition	A temporary increase in the strength of an extinguished response caused by an unrelated stimulus event is referred to as disinhibition.
Personality trait	According to the Diagnostic and Statistical Manual of the American Psychiatric Association, a personality trait is a "prominent aspect of personality that is exhibited in a wide range of important social and personal contexts. ...".
Emotion	An emotion is a mental states that arise spontaneously, rather than through conscious effort. They are often accompanied by physiological changes.
Mental processes	The thoughts, feelings, and motives that each of us experiences privately but that cannot be observed directly are called mental processes.
IQ test	An IQ test is a standardized test developed to measure a person's cognitive abilities ("intelligence") in relation to their age group.
Correlation	A statistical technique for determining the degree of association between two or more variables is referred to as correlation.
Reasoning	Reasoning is the act of using reason to derive a conclusion from certain premises. There are two main methods to reach a conclusion, deductive reasoning and inductive reasoning.
Habit	A habit is a response that has become completely separated from its eliciting stimulus. Early learning theorists used the term to describe S-R associations, however not all S-R associations become a habit, rather many are extinguished after reinforcement is withdrawn.
Divergent thinking	A thought process that attempts to generate multiple solutions to problems is called divergent thinking.
Stages	Stages represent relatively discrete periods of time in which functioning is qualitatively different from functioning at other periods.
Socialization	Social rules and social relations are created, communicated, and changed in verbal and nonverbal ways creating social complexity useful in identifying outsiders and intelligent breeding partners. The process of learning these skills is called socialization.
Self-image	A person's self-image is the mental picture, generally of a kind that is quite resistant to change, that depicts not only details that are potentially available to objective investigation by others, but also items that have been learned by that person about himself or herself.
Nurture	Nurture refers to the environmental influences on behavior due to nutrition, culture, socioeconomic status, and learning.
Perception	Perception is the process of acquiring, interpreting, selecting, and organizing sensory information.
Evolution	Commonly used to refer to gradual change, evolution is the change in the frequency of alleles within a population from one generation to the next. This change may be caused by different mechanisms, including natural selection, genetic drift, or changes in population (gene flow).
Knowledge base	The general background information a person possesses, which influences most cognitive task performance is called the knowledge base.
Elaboration	The extensiveness of processing at any given level of memory is called elaboration. The use of elaboration changes developmentally. Adolescents are more likely to use elaboration

Chapter 12. From Curiosity to Creativity

Chapter 12. From Curiosity to Creativity

	spontaneously than children.
Neuron	The neuron is the primary cell of the nervous system. They are found in the brain, the spinal cord, in the nerves and ganglia of the peripheral nervous system. It is a specialized cell that conducts impulses through the nervous system and contains three major parts: cell body, dendrites, and an axon. It can have many dendrites but only one axon.
Insight	Insight refers to a sudden awareness of the relationships among various elements that had previously appeared to be independent of one another.
Problem solving	An attempt to find an appropriate way of attaining a goal when the goal is not readily available is called problem solving.
Self-reflection	In Bandura's social cognitive theory, the ability to analyze one's thoughts and actions is referred to as self-reflection.
Brainstorming	Brainstorming is an organized approach for producing ideas by letting the mind think without interruption. The term was coined by Alex Osborn.
Automaticity	The ability to process information with little or no effort is referred to as automaticity.
Intuition	Quick, impulsive thought that does not make use of formal logic or clear reasoning is referred to as intuition.

Chapter 12. From Curiosity to Creativity

Chapter 13. Need for Control, Mastery, and Self-Esteem

Emotion	An emotion is a mental states that arise spontaneously, rather than through conscious effort. They are often accompanied by physiological changes.
Anxiety	Anxiety is a complex combination of the feeling of fear, apprehension and worry often accompanied by physical sensations such as palpitations, chest pain and/or shortness of breath.
Depression	In everyday language depression refers to any downturn in mood, which may be relatively transitory and perhaps due to something trivial. This is differentiated from Clinical depression which is marked by symptoms that last two weeks or more and are so severe that they interfere with daily living.
Self-esteem	Self-esteem refers to a person's subjective appraisal of himself or herself as intrinsically positive or negative to some degree.
Variable	A variable refers to a measurable factor, characteristic, or attribute of an individual or a system.
Addiction	Addiction is an uncontrollable compulsion to repeat a behavior regardless of its consequences. Many drugs or behaviors can precipitate a pattern of conditions recognized as addiction, which include a craving for more of the drug or behavior, increased physiological tolerance to exposure, and withdrawal symptoms in the absence of the stimulus.
Eating disorders	Psychological disorders characterized by distortion of the body image and gross disturbances in eating patterns are called eating disorders.
Aversive stimulus	A stimulus that elicits pain, fear, or avoidance is an aversive stimulus.
Stimulus	A change in an environmental condition that elicits a response is a stimulus.
Cardiovascular disease	Cardiovascular disease refers to afflictions in the mechanisms, including the heart, blood vessels, and their controllers, that are responsible for transporting blood to the body's tissues and organs. Psychological factors may play important roles in such diseases and their treatments.
Stages	Stages represent relatively discrete periods of time in which functioning is qualitatively different from functioning at other periods.
Chronic	Chronic refers to a relatively long duration, usually more than a few months.
Immune response	The body's defensive reaction to invasion by bacteria, viral agents, or other foreign substances is called the immune response.
Immune system	The most important function of the human immune system occurs at the cellular level of the blood and tissues. The lymphatic and blood circulation systems are highways for specialized white blood cells. These cells include B cells, T cells, natural killer cells, and macrophages. All function with the primary objective of recognizing, attacking and destroying bacteria, viruses, cancer cells, and all substances seen as foreign.
Locus of control	The place to which an individual attributes control over the receiving of reinforcers -either inside or outside the self is referred to as locus of control.
Genetics	Genetics is the science of genes, heredity, and the variation of organisms.
Variance	The degree to which scores differ among individuals in a distribution of scores is the variance.
Learning	Learning is a relatively permanent change in behavior that results from experience. Thus, to attribute a behavioral change to learning, the change must be relatively permanent and must result from experience.

Chapter 13. Need for Control, Mastery, and Self-Esteem

Chapter 13. Need for Control, Mastery, and Self-Esteem

Cognition	The intellectual processes through which information is obtained, transformed, stored, retrieved, and otherwise used is cognition.
Personality	Personality refers to the pattern of enduring characteristics that differentiates a person, the patterns of behaviors that make each individual unique.
Reinforcement Theory	Reinforcement theory holds that reinforcers can control behavior. The definition has two main components: Contingency, where the occurrence of the reinforcer depends on the occurrence of the learner's response, and Rate of Responding, where the reinforcer serves to increase the learner's rate of responding.
Reinforcement	In operant conditioning, reinforcement is any change in an environment that (a) occurs after the behavior, (b) seems to make that behavior re-occur more often in the future and (c) that reoccurence of behavior must be the result of the change.
Individualism	Individualism refers to putting personal goals ahead of group goals and defining one's identity in terms of personal attributes rather than group memberships.
Meditation	Meditation usually refers to a state in which the body is consciously relaxed and the mind is allowed to become calm and focused.
Theories	Theories are logically self-consistent models or frameworks describing the behavior of a certain natural or social phenomenon. They are broad explanations and predictions concerning phenomena of interest.
Biofeedback	Biofeedback is the process of measuring and quantifying an aspect of a subject's physiology, analyzing the data, and then feeding back the information to the subject in a form that allows the subject to enact physiological change.
Attitude	An enduring mental representation of a person, place, or thing that evokes an emotional response and related behavior is called attitude.
Wisdom	Wisdom is the ability to make correct judgments and decisions. It is an intangible quality gained through experience. Whether or not something is wise is determined in a pragmatic sense by its popularity, how long it has been around, and its ability to predict against future events.
Behavioral control	Behavioral control refers to the contingencies that determine the expression of a behavior through manipulations of reinforcement and punishment.
Social skills	Social skills are skills used to interact and communicate with others to assist status in the social structure and other motivations.
Motivation	In psychology, motivation is the driving force (desire) behind all actions of an organism.
Achievement motive	The need to master difficult challenges, to outperform others, and to meet high standards of excellence is called the achievement motive.
Thematic Apperception Test	The Thematic Apperception Test uses a standard series of provocative yet ambiguous pictures about which the subject must tell a story. Each story is carefully analyzed to uncover underlying needs, attitudes, and patterns of reaction.
Apperception	A newly experienced sensation is related to past experiences to form an understood situation. For Wundt, consciousness is composed of two "stages:" There is a large capacity working memory called the Blickfeld and the narrower consciousness called Apperception, or selective attention.
Motives	Needs or desires that energize and direct behavior toward a goal are motives.
Validity	The extent to which a test measures what it is intended to measure is called validity.
Brain	The brain controls and coordinates most movement, behavior and homeostatic body functions

Chapter 13. Need for Control, Mastery, and Self-Esteem

Chapter 13. Need for Control, Mastery, and Self-Esteem

	such as heartbeat, blood pressure, fluid balance and body temperature. Functions of the brain are responsible for cognition, emotion, memory, motor learning and other sorts of learning. The brain is primarily made up of two types of cells: glia and neurons.
Neurotransmitter	A neurotransmitter is a chemical that is used to relay, amplify and modulate electrical signals between a neurons and another cell.
Incentive	An incentive is what is expected once a behavior is performed. An incentive acts as a reinforcer.
Affect	A subjective feeling or emotional tone often accompanied by bodily expressions noticeable to others is called affect.
Behavioral inhibition system	The behavioral inhibition system is a circuit in the limbic system that responds to threat signals by inhibiting activity and causing anxiety.
Behavioral inhibition	Physiological probes of children with behavioral inhibition show significantly higher measures of activity in the sympathetic nervous system and hypothalamic-pituitary axis than in non-inhibited children. Kagan postulates that anxiety-prone children are born with a lower firing threshold in amygdala and hypothalamic neurons. His work provides a robust model for predicting temperamental forerunners of anxiety disorders.
Attention	Attention is the cognitive process of selectively concentrating on one thing while ignoring other things. Psychologists have labeled three types of attention: sustained attention, selective attention, and divided attention.
Social learning theory	Social learning theory explains the process of gender typing in terms of observation, imitation, and role playing .
Social learning	Social learning is learning that occurs as a function of observing, retaining and replicating behavior observed in others. Although social learning can occur at any stage in life, it is thought to be particularly important during childhood, particularly as authority becomes important.
Modeling	A type of behavior learned through observation of others demonstrating the same behavior is modeling.
Internalization	The developmental change from behavior that is externally controlled to behavior that is controlled by internal standards and principles is referred to as internalization.
Need for achievement	Need for Achievement is a term introduced by David McClelland into the field of psychology, referring to an individual's desire for significant accomplishment, mastering of skills, control, or high standards.
Coding	In senation, coding is the process by which information about the quality and quantity of a stimulus is preserved in the pattern of action potentials sent through sensory neurons to the central nervous system.
Construct	A generalized concept, such as anxiety or gravity, is a construct.
Achievement motivation	The psychological need in humans for success is called achievement motivation.
Incentive value	The value of a goal above and beyond its ability to fill a need is its incentive value.
Nervous system	The body's electrochemical communication circuitry, made up of billions of neurons is a nervous system.
Self-image	A person's self-image is the mental picture, generally of a kind that is quite resistant to change, that depicts not only details that are potentially available to objective

Chapter 13. Need for Control, Mastery, and Self-Esteem

Chapter 13. Need for Control, Mastery, and Self-Esteem

	investigation by others, but also items that have been learned by that person about himself or herself.
Feedback	Feedback refers to information returned to a person about the effects a response has had.
Intrinsic motivation	Intrinsic motivation causes people to engage in an activity for its own sake. They are subjective factors and include self-determination, curiosity, challenge, effort, and others.
Mastery orientation	According to Dweck, mastery orientation is an outlook in which individuals focus on the task rather than on their ability, have positive affect, and generate solution-oriented strategies that improve their performance.
Self-efficacy	Self-efficacy is the belief that one has the capabilities to execute the courses of actions required to manage prospective situations.
Goal-directed behavior	Goal-directed behavior is means-end problem solving behavior. In the infant, such behavior is first observed in the latter part of the first year.
Statistic	A statistic is an observable random variable of a sample.
Performance orientation	Performance orientation is an outlook in which individuals are concerned with performance outcome rather than performance process. For performance-oriented students, winning is what matters.
Perception	Perception is the process of acquiring, interpreting, selecting, and organizing sensory information.
Trait	An enduring personality characteristic that tends to lead to certain behaviors is called a trait. The term trait also means a genetically inherited feature of an organism.
Autonomy	Autonomy is the condition of something that does not depend on anything else.
Negative feedback	In negative feedback, the output of a system is added back into the input, so as to reverse the direction of change. This tends to keep the output from changing, so it is stabilizing and attempts to maintain homeostasis.
Guilt	Guilt describes many concepts related to a negative emotion or condition caused by actions which are believed to be, morally wrong. According to Freud, the avoidance of guilt is the basis for moral behavior.
Reflection	Reflection is the process of rephrasing or repeating thoughts and feelings expressed, making the person more aware of what they are saying or thinking.
Adolescence	The period of life bounded by puberty and the assumption of adult responsibilities is adolescence.
Gender difference	A gender difference is a disparity between genders involving quality or quantity. Though some gender differences are controversial, they are not to be confused with sexist stereotypes.
Self-concept	Self-concept refers to domain-specific evaluations of the self where a domain may be academics, athletics, etc.
Individual differences	Individual differences psychology studies the ways in which individual people differ in their behavior. This is distinguished from other aspects of psychology in that although psychology is ostensibly a study of individuals, modern psychologists invariably study groups.
Nurture	Nurture refers to the environmental influences on behavior due to nutrition, culture, socioeconomic status, and learning.

Chapter 13. Need for Control, Mastery, and Self-Esteem

Chapter 14. Self-Regulation of Motivation

Learning	Learning is a relatively permanent change in behavior that results from experience. Thus, to attribute a behavioral change to learning, the change must be relatively permanent and must result from experience.
Cognition	The intellectual processes through which information is obtained, transformed, stored, retrieved, and otherwise used is cognition.
Theories	Theories are logically self-consistent models or frameworks describing the behavior of a certain natural or social phenomenon. They are broad explanations and predictions concerning phenomena of interest.
Social skills	Social skills are skills used to interact and communicate with others to assist status in the social structure and other motivations.
Construct	A generalized concept, such as anxiety or gravity, is a construct.
Friendship	The essentials of friendship are reciprocity and commitment between individuals who see themselves more or less as equals. Interaction between friends rests on a more equal power base than the interaction between children and adults.
Motivation	In psychology, motivation is the driving force (desire) behind all actions of an organism.
Consciousness	The awareness of the sensations, thoughts, and feelings being experienced at a given moment is called consciousness.
Evolutionary perspective	A perspective that focuses on how humans have evolved and adapted behaviors required for survival against various environmental pressures over the long course is called the evolutionary perspective.
Receptor	A sensory receptor is a structure that recognizes a stimulus in the internal or external environment of an organism. In response to stimuli the sensory receptor initiates sensory transduction by creating graded potentials or action potentials in the same cell or in an adjacent one.
Long-term memory	Long-term memory is memory that lasts from over 30 seconds to years.
Forebrain	The forebrain is the highest level of the brain. Key structures in the forebrain are the limbic system, thalamus, basal ganglia, hypothalamus, and cerebral cortex.
Creativity	Creativity is the ability to think about something in novel and unusual ways and come up with unique solutions to problems. It involves divergent thinking, having many solutions or views to a problem.
Working Memory	Working memory is the collection of structures and processes in the brain used for temporarily storing and manipulating information. Working memory consists of both memory for items that are currently being processed, and components governing attention and directing the processing itself.
Adaptation	Adaptation is a lowering of sensitivity to a stimulus following prolonged exposure to that stimulus. Behavioral adaptations are special ways a particular organism behaves to survive in its natural habitat.
Brain	The brain controls and coordinates most movement, behavior and homeostatic body functions such as heartbeat, blood pressure, fluid balance and body temperature. Functions of the brain are responsible for cognition, emotion, memory, motor learning and other sorts of learning. The brain is primarily made up of two types of cells: glia and neurons.
Gene	A gene is an ultramicroscopic area of the chromosome. It is the smallest physical unit of the DNA molecule that carries a piece of hereditary information.
Evolution	Commonly used to refer to gradual change, evolution is the change in the frequency of alleles

Chapter 14. Self-Regulation of Motivation

Chapter 14. Self-Regulation of Motivation

	within a population from one generation to the next. This change may be caused by different mechanisms, including natural selection, genetic drift, or changes in population (gene flow).
Emotion	An emotion is a mental states that arise spontaneously, rather than through conscious effort. They are often accompanied by physiological changes.
Attention	Attention is the cognitive process of selectively concentrating on one thing while ignoring other things. Psychologists have labeled three types of attention: sustained attention, selective attention, and divided attention.
Anecdotal evidence	Anecdotal evidence is unreliable evidence based on personal experience that has not been empirically tested, and which is often used in an argument as if it had been scientifically or statistically proven. The person using anecdotal evidence may or may not be aware of the fact that, by doing so, they are generalizing.
Free choice	Free choice refers to the ability to freely make choices that are not controlled by genetics, learning, or unconscious forces.
Superordinate goal	Superordinate goal refers to a goal that exceeds or overrides all others; a goal that renders other goals relatively less important.
Superordinate	A hypernym is a word whose extension includes the extension of the word of which it is a hypernym. A word that is more generic or broad than another given word. Another term for a hypernym is a superordinate.
Self-esteem	Self-esteem refers to a person's subjective appraisal of himself or herself as intrinsically positive or negative to some degree.
Feedback	Feedback refers to information returned to a person about the effects a response has had.
Variable	A variable refers to a measurable factor, characteristic, or attribute of an individual or a system.
Self-efficacy	Self-efficacy is the belief that one has the capabilities to execute the courses of actions required to manage prospective situations.
Personality	Personality refers to the pattern of enduring characteristics that differentiates a person, the patterns of behaviors that make each individual unique.
Social psychology	Social psychology is the study of the nature and causes of human social behavior, with an emphasis on how people think towards each other and how they relate to each other.
Ego	In Freud's view the Ego serves to balance our primitive needs and our moral beliefs and taboos. Relying on experience, a healthy Ego provides the ability to adapt to reality and interact with the outside world.
Goal-directed behavior	Goal-directed behavior is means-end problem solving behavior. In the infant, such behavior is first observed in the latter part of the first year.
Individual differences	Individual differences psychology studies the ways in which individual people differ in their behavior. This is distinguished from other aspects of psychology in that although psychology is ostensibly a study of individuals, modern psychologists invariably study groups.
Motivational processes	In observational learning, the motivational processes are the degree to which a behavior is seen to result in a valued outcome (expectancies) will influence the likelihood that one will adopt a modeled behavior .
Anxiety	Anxiety is a complex combination of the feeling of fear, apprehension and worry often accompanied by physical sensations such as palpitations, chest pain and/or shortness of breath.
Automaticity	The ability to process information with little or no effort is referred to as automaticity.

Chapter 14. Self-Regulation of Motivation

Chapter 14. Self-Regulation of Motivation

Unconscious thought	Unconscious thought is Freud's concept of a reservoir of unacceptable wishes, feelings, and thoughts that are beyond conscious awareness.
Subjective experience	Subjective experience refers to reality as it is perceived and interpreted, not as it exists objectively.
Simulation	A simulation is an imitation of some real device or state of affairs. Simulation attempts to represent certain features of the behavior of a physical or abstract system by the behavior of another system.
Motives	Needs or desires that energize and direct behavior toward a goal are motives.
Positive relationship	Statistically, a positive relationship refers to a mathematical relationship in which increases in one measure are matched by increases in the other.
Placebo effect	The placebo effect is the phenomenon that a patient's symptoms can be alleviated by an otherwise ineffective treatment, apparently because the individual expects or believes that it will work.
Placebo	Placebo refers to a bogus treatment that has the appearance of being genuine.
Psychoactive drug	A psychoactive drug or psychotropic substance is a chemical that alters brain function, resulting in temporary changes in perception, mood, consciousness, or behavior. Such drugs are often used for recreational and spiritual purposes, as well as in medicine, especially for treating neurological and psychological illnesses.
Depression	In everyday language depression refers to any downturn in mood, which may be relatively transitory and perhaps due to something trivial. This is differentiated from Clinical depression which is marked by symptoms that last two weeks or more and are so severe that they interfere with daily living.
Reasoning	Reasoning is the act of using reason to derive a conclusion from certain premises. There are two main methods to reach a conclusion, deductive reasoning and inductive reasoning.
Experimental group	Experimental group refers to any group receiving a treatment effect in an experiment.
Antidepressants	Antidepressants are medications used primarily in the treatment of clinical depression. Antidepressants create little if any immediate change in mood and require between several days and several weeks to take effect.
Antidepressant	An antidepressant is a medication used primarily in the treatment of clinical depression. They are not thought to produce tolerance, although sudden withdrawal may produce adverse effects. They create little if any immediate change in mood and require between several days and several weeks to take effect.
Test anxiety	High levels of arousal and worry that seriously impair test performance is referred to as test anxiety.
Perception	Perception is the process of acquiring, interpreting, selecting, and organizing sensory information.
Problem solving	An attempt to find an appropriate way of attaining a goal when the goal is not readily available is called problem solving.
Cognitive restructuring	Cognitive restructuring refers to any behavior therapy procedure that attempts to alter the manner in which a client thinks about life so that he or she changes overt behavior and emotions.
Evolutionary psychology	Evolutionary psychology proposes that cognition and behavior can be better understood in light of evolutionary history.

Chapter 14. Self-Regulation of Motivation

Self-concept	Self-concept refers to domain-specific evaluations of the self where a domain may be academics, athletics, etc.
Attitude	An enduring mental representation of a person, place, or thing that evokes an emotional response and related behavior is called attitude.
Affect	A subjective feeling or emotional tone often accompanied by bodily expressions noticeable to others is called affect.
Creative self	According to Alfred Adler, the self-aware aspect of personality that strives to achieve its full potential is referred to as the creative self.
Alcoholic	An alcoholic is dependent on alcohol as characterized by craving, loss of control, physical dependence and withdrawal symptoms, and tolerance.
Possible self	What individuals might become, what they would like to become, and what they are afraid of becoming is called the possible self.
Elaboration	The extensiveness of processing at any given level of memory is called elaboration. The use of elaboration changes developmentally. Adolescents are more likely to use elaboration spontaneously than children.
Trait	An enduring personality characteristic that tends to lead to certain behaviors is called a trait. The term trait also means a genetically inherited feature of an organism.
Prototype	A concept of a category of objects or events that serves as a good example of the category is called a prototype.
Negative affectivity	Negative affectivity is a personality variable that refers to a tendency to experience negative emotions across many different situations.
Deprivation	Deprivation, is the loss or withholding of normal stimulation, nutrition, comfort, love, and so forth; a condition of lacking. The level of stimulation is less than what is required.
Neuroticism	Eysenck's use of the term neuroticism (or Emotional Stability) was proposed as the dimension describing individual differences in the predisposition towards neurotic disorder.
Sensation	Sensation is the first stage in the chain of biochemical and neurologic events that begins with the impinging of a stimulus upon the receptor cells of a sensory organ, which then leads to perception, the mental state that is reflected in statements like "I see a uniformly blue wall."
Norms	In testing, standards of test performance that permit the comparison of one person's score on the test to the scores of others who have taken the same test are referred to as norms.
Sensation seeking	A generalized preference for high or low levels of sensory stimulation is referred to as sensation seeking.
Survey	A method of scientific investigation in which a large sample of people answer questions about their attitudes or behavior is referred to as a survey.
Questionnaire	A self-report method of data collection or clinical assessment method in which the individual being studied checks off items on a printed list, answers multiple-choice questions, or writes out answers to essay questions aimed at producing a selfdescription is called questionnaire.
Factor analysis	Factor analysis is a statistical technique that originated in psychometrics. The objective is to explain the most of the variability among a number of observable random variables in terms of a smaller number of unobservable random variables called factors.
Individualism	Individualism refers to putting personal goals ahead of group goals and defining one's identity in terms of personal attributes rather than group memberships.

Chapter 14. Self-Regulation of Motivation

Chapter 14. Self-Regulation of Motivation

Autonomy	Autonomy is the condition of something that does not depend on anything else.
Shaping	The concept of reinforcing successive, increasingly accurate approximations to a target behavior is called shaping. The target behavior is broken down into a hierarchy of elemental steps, each step more sophisticated then the last. By successively reinforcing each of the the elemental steps, a form of differential reinforcement, until that step is learned while extinguishing the step below, the target behavior is gradually achieved.
Modeling	A type of behavior learned through observation of others demonstrating the same behavior is modeling.
Mastery orientation	According to Dweck, mastery orientation is an outlook in which individuals focus on the task rather than on their ability, have positive affect, and generate solution-oriented strategies that improve their performance.
Performance orientation	Performance orientation is an outlook in which individuals are concerned with performance outcome rather than performance process. For performance-oriented students, winning is what matters.
Reflection	Reflection is the process of rephrasing or repeating thoughts and feelings expressed, making the person more aware of what they are saying or thinking.
Personality trait	According to the Diagnostic and Statistical Manual of the American Psychiatric Association, a personality trait is a "prominent aspect of personality that is exhibited in a wide range of important social and personal contexts. ...".
Self-awareness	Realization that one's existence and functioning are separate from those of other people and things is called self-awareness.

Chapter 14. Self-Regulation of Motivation

BF
503
.F72

00050263 1

SOUTH UNIVERSITY LIBRARY

Printed in the United States
75288LV00003B/63